THE MILLENNIUM HOTEL

Wesleyan Poetry

Other Books by Mark Rudman

POETRY:

By Contraries
The Nowhere Steps
Rider

CHAPBOOKS:

In the Neighboring Cell
The Mystery in the Garden
The Ruin Revived

PROSE:

Robert Lowell: An Introduction to the Poetry
Diverse Voices: Essays on Poets and Poetry
Realm of Unknowing

TRANSLATION:

My Sister—Life and the Highest Sickness, poems by Boris Pasternak
(with Bohdan Boychuk)
Square of Angels: The Selected Poems of Bohdan Antonych
(with Bohdan Boychuk)
Memories of Love: The Selected Poems of Bohdan Boychuk
Euripides' Daughters of Troy

Mark Rudman

❧

THE

MILLENNIUM

HOTEL

Wesleyan University Press

Published by University Press of New England

Hanover and London

For my father Charles Kenneth Rudman

and my son Samuel Hardie Rudman

Wesleyan University Press

University Press of New England, Hanover, NH 03755

© 1996 by Mark Rudman

All rights reserved

Printed in the United States of America

5 4 3 2 1

CIP data appear at the end of the book

Grateful acknowledgment is made to the editors of the magazines and anthologies in which sections of this book first appeared:

"Mixed Messages," *The Alembic*; "Aesacus, The Diver," "Aesacus Risen," *Arion;* "Gratuitous Act," "Semaphore," *Boulevard*; "Wood Floors (1,2)," *Colorado Review*; "Poolside," *Columbia Magazine*; "On the Wheel Of," "Pool Hall," *Crab Orchard Review;* "Easter Weekend in Denver," *Denver Quarterly;* "Role Play (after Horace)," *Partisan Review*; "*In the torrent* (after Johannes Bobrowski)," "Motel En Route to 'Life Out There,'" *Pequod;* "Above and Below in Mexico," *Ploughshares*; "Love's Way," *Yellow Silk.*

The following poems appeared in these anthologies: "Aesacus, The Diver" in *After Ovid,* edited by Michael Hoffman and James Lasdun, Farrar, Strauss & Giroux; "Screen Image," *The Killing Spirit,* Overlook Press; "Waterfall (after Pierre Reverdy)" in *20th Century French Poetry,* edited by Paul Auster, Random House.

I would also like to thank Carol Ardman, Christopher Benfey, Ted Blanchard, Lawrence Joseph, and Katharine Washburn for their careful readings and encouragement.

The publisher gratefully acknowledges the support of Lannan Foundation in the publication of this book.

Contents

I   SCREEN IMAGE

Birthday Blues   3
Screen Image: (Royal Emerald Hotel, Nassau)   9
Gratuitous Act   12
Role Play (after Horace)   15
Distracted in Beverly Hills   18

II   THE MILLENNIUM HOTEL

The Millennium Hotel   25
  1. Prologue and Lament   25
  2. Nothing Seasonal   27
  3. The Path   29
  4. Stormwatch   33
  5. The Millenium   37
  6. *"Around this time you began making transcontinental flights
     alone."*   43
  7. After the Storm   45
  8. "And What If It Had Been His Last Wish . . ."   46
  9. The Stewardess   48
  10. The Heights   50
  11. 1812   53
  12. "Our beautiful mothers! Death isn't . . ."   57
  13. Walker's Pond   58
  14. Semaphore   59
  15. Night Thoughts (after Heinrich Heine)   67
  16. "Succulents subjected—"   69
  17. "How far can we take chance, can chance take us?" 71
  18. (Pause.)   75
  19. March (after Boris Pasternak)   78
  20. *In the torrent* (after Johannes Bobrowski)   80
  21. Pool Hall   82
  22. Before Summer Rain (after Rainer Maria Rilke)   84

23. Poolside   85
24. Gorge   93

III MOTEL EN ROUTE TO "LIFE OUT THERE"

Wood Floors   97
Love's Way   104
Love's Mirrors   114
Set Design   117
Soho: The Early Days   121
Easter Weekend in Denver   125
On the Wheel Of   134
Aesacus, the Diver (after Ovid)   145
Aesacus Risen   149
Aesacus and the Dancer   151
Mixed Messages   152
Motel En Route to "Life Out There"   164

IV ABOVE AND BELOW

Above and Below in Mexico   177

Notes   185

I

❧

SCREEN IMAGE

BIRTHDAY BLUES

Today's the rider's birthday.

I see you're already lower-casing him . . .

Would you rather I . . .

What is this "I." You have none.

Today's the rider's birthday.

Except he's dead.

In a contrary mood today?

Not in the way you'd think.

I'm your friend, remember? And I can't hurt you. I have no body.

Neither does Krang.

K——?

The bodiless brain. The Ninja Turtles' nemesis. The guy who oversees
all of their activities.

*And yet you carry him in your pocket like a good luck charm. You perplex
your son who can't see the humor in your perversity because to him Krang is
just, to put it plainly, disgusting.*

Just his brain. On the show and the Nintendo game his naked
brain is always
      safely encased within
        a robot's body

where his stomach
      and not his head
        ought to be.

Ought? I thought we had done with the realm of could-have-been. The realm of shoulds.

Who is ever done with—anything?
Just because I agree with Marie-Louise Von Franz's
          imprecation
          "no more shoulds"
doesn't mean I'm freed from the   actuality.

And just because the rider is dead
doesn't mean that today isn't
his birthday.

April 17. I'm fine, really.

I believe you.

But the week has been—.

I know. But think of it this way: you're lucky that you can break down.

I kept scratching my brain in imagination trying to remember if this was the week when B died a year ago. And J the same week the year before.

After each death something went wrong with your body.

All right, all right. Even though I had the flu I dragged myself to the gym to stretch out on the mats and listen to some calming music on my Walkman. This was going well. I had my arms and legs extended as far as possible in the opposite direction and I could feel my lungs release . . . , but when I reached for my toes I . . . convulsed and burst into tears.

Good thing you'd worn your sunglasses.

Yeah. I knew that the tears could have been mistaken for sweat and the groans for . . .

and while it was days before the date, as if emblazoned (would stare me down-to-distraction) I just could not stop thinking about the intimate

4

quiet moments we shared; our rare and wonderful moments of true soli-
tude together . . . ; the unforced gentleness and sense of mutuality . . . :

Buber . . .

That's *so* unimportant. The point is that he had internalized the lessons;
it was in his nature to be that way.

*I don't see what's so strange. His birthday was approaching. You were sad.
That's perfectly normal.*

But what pierced me at that moment like an ax was the recognition
that I never had
      a   conversation with my (blood) father.

Don't be dumbfounded. My feelings about the two men are always in
dialogue, crissing and crossing.

Lying in that relaxed position on the exercise mat
listening to the intervals
in Ry Cooder's mesmerizing *Paris, Texas* score, it
              hit me that as my father's
birthday approached, or the hour
of his suicide neared,
that I felt mildly aware, mildly   sad,
but not remotely devastated and torn that I had lost

someone with whom I had an intimacy that could

never be repeated.

Nothing can—.

You know I don't mean it that way.

Then be precise.

Someone who, at least at crucial times, communicated a warmth and
love and care without

*competing with you and undercutting you at every instant like
your blood father. And your grandfather—.*

Thanks.

That's what I'm here for.

So I was torn by a new perplexity with regard to my real father. I never
lived with him but we spent countless hours alone together and he was
often, before he hit the bottle, quite friendly, easy-going, low pressure.

A compañero.

We liked to hobo around together.

But even looking at clusters of the best moments we had in each
other's presence we still never had
                        a conversation. He had his
mind made up about me and, with his game-plan fully laid out,
chose to employ this or that tactic to
                    edify, or instruct . . . , to
lead me onto better paths

for I am in no way criticizing his motivation in trying to help
me
        GROW

it was just that he had no

        EARS

He knew in advance anything I could possibly think or say.

*But it wasn't personal. It was just the way he was. You brought
a friend to dinner who was stationed on a ship outside Nankeng
Harbor. Your father appeared to listen to his sea stories
   —and the thing that "most blew his mind"—
     when the missile, launched
   from the ship, landed
        "directly on"*

a peasant hoeing rice who "didn't know where the hell
        he was going"
and blew him away completely
and the sailors laughed

    —and your friend came apart—

and while your FACE *showed proper astonishment*
        your FATHER
    just pawed the place mat

    to rid it of imaginary crumbs

    and with stern and solemn nods

    that withheld surprise at all costs

and gravity of tone worthy of Lincoln!

told your friend that the gist   of war was   boredom

and he, perhaps unused to such practiced delivery during
"informal" gatherings

took this in then whispered wide-eyed that he could not believe
how your father could know everything he'd gone through
when he'd never gone through it

and while his sadism was not in full flower in such isolated
instances it was

a drag.

No wonder I was touched when Sam agreed to an evening of five-card-
stud on one condition: "no poker-faces"!

Your father's mask was his face.

No—depth? Interior—life?

No—but that he cared more about the impression he made than about what you or your friend were undergoing.

He was always onstage, your father. Preening for posterity in a void of his own invention.

Ok.

He was never, or always and only, himself.

SCREEN IMAGE:
(ROYAL EMERALD HOTEL, NASSAU)

Viciousness incarnate. Meanness engraved.
Boneless, atomic, he leaned on the swivel

stool. His back to the bar.
To the gilded mirrors inhabited

by a jagged skyline, bottles;
gold labels: Chivas, Cointreau, Cutty Sark. . . .

Anyone would have noted this presence
even if the man had been

no one, but with his initials
in red on shirt-cuffs, cuff-links,

lapels, blazer breast-pocket, and socks,
it seemed almost disingenuous

for the boy to ask "Are you—?"—
but it was the best he could do.

Sloe-eyed, conspiratorial, the actor spoke
out of the side of his mouth

but his gravelly menacing bass
carried kind words. "Pleased to meet you

son. Would you—mind—if I—bought—you a drink?
Bartender—get the boy a—'Shirley'—"

and then he winked!—a—'Roy Rogers.'"
They drank in dark and blissful silence.

"Just do me one favor, son; don't tell anyone
you saw me. I'm here . . . to get away."

The warm and intimate way the actor delivered these words
made the boy keen to keep a vow . . . of silence;

to ignore his chance to shine in the rec-room among the jaded kids
who'd waste no time making sure everyone who could know would
      know;

no, he would not tell that freckled snot from Great Neck
who came to Nassau with his own ping pong racquet. . . .

The actor's equally glamorous friends,
who'd entered without a sound,

pressed the rims of cocktail glasses to their lips;
knocked down their martinis in one

gulp; hissed: retracted their chins like cobras.
The leather armrests on the bar let out a gasp

which led the two women to exchange quick
I didn't do it, did you? glances,

as if their rigid posture and breathless
diaphragms betrayed them, along

with their volitionless nylon rustling. . . .
They were prisoners anyway:

of masklike makeup; tintinnabulating bracelets;
miniscule purses without shoulder straps

and strapless, tight-waisted dresses; umbrella-spined bras;
nylons, garters, girdles, high heels: glued hair.

(Was the woman who was "with" the actor
reciting a silent mantra

that he himself would never do anything
like hurl boiling coffee in her face

as he did to Gloria Graham
in *The Big Heat?*)

Silken and silver were the hair and suit and voice
of the man who uttered the actor's first name.

Wouldn't "our table's ready" have been sufficient?
The actor dispersed like liquid mercury—

too early in time to draw some wry pleasure
from the uncanny resemblance

between the "special effect" on celluloid
and his own flesh and blood.

The boy did not move but eyed the party
through the speckled mirror; and though

he was as aware as any American
that whatever the actor hadn't done

in real life or was yet to do,
like push the future

President out of a speeding coupe in *The Killers* . . .
that he owed his renown to the brazen, indomitable cop

he played on *M-Squad*, the boy saw him repeatedly
as the itinerant cruelty in *The Missouri Traveller*

who lashed that boy's back in the heat-stricken barn
for feeding the skeletal horses extra hay.

He couldn't remember why he and his father
had gone to this bleak, obscure "sleeper" anyway,

unless, alone together in a place he could not remember,
they had time to kill.

GRATUITOUS ACT

Dawn had scarcely broken when *because those kids*
he went to school with in that hick town
would kill to be in his shoes now, he said
"ok" to a day of deep-sea fishing:
his father's heaven, his abyss
of boredom and panic, trapped
among strangers hellbent on pleasure;
the ghastly sultry stillness,
the timeless, eternal, waiting—
broken only by a cry that went out every time
we passed another rig, "catch anything?"
He had some Cherry Bombs in his pocket,
burning to be used: could he hurl one
onto an approaching boat?

In the tireless, omnipresent dampness
he set a match to the wick: it did not seem
to react; sizzle, give off
any light; yet some purposive
silent and invisible flame must have crawled
down the stem to get it to ignite in his hand—
which went instantly black.
Like charred paper.

The captain went below deck and came back up
soot-blackened from the axle grease
he'd scraped from the engine.
He rubbed it on the boy's palm.
The pain went away instantly.
The blackness remained.

How long would he have to wait
for the hotel nurse to wind
the white gauze bandage around his wound?
It should have been enough to earn him a night alone
in their room . . . but he was still recovering
when he and his father, his friend and his father,

jumped into a rachitic taxi which hung an abrupt
right onto an unmarked road and roared
down a narrow, sandy path,
where thorns and branches closed in,
scratching, beating it back, so that his party
could listen to the bongos and the castanets
on the floodlit, open-air dance floor.

The boys drank "Roy Rogers,"
and chewed the stems of maraschino cherries.
The women, seated alone together, had
all the right body language: it would never
enter anyone's mind that they weren't
having the best of times. *Of course* the boys
(two non-threatening pre-adolescents
playing at being men) *could join them.*
They'd been alone a long time
before the women thought to ask
where they came from, who they were with.

That was the boys' cue to guide their eyes toward the two
bachelors through the smoke of the room—
(to which their "Havana's" were contributing—)
men who, "combining style and comfort,"
might have stepped out of *GQ* in their lightweight,
"tropical" blazers, white trousers, and Pima cotton shirts.
It had taken him a while to warm to Rube,
his new friend's lawyer father: his crewcut and bow ties;
his mimicry in the shrewd, digressive jokes he told
where Jewish vampires scoffed in Yinglish
as their hapless prey brandished useless crosses. . . .

The tall Bahamian entered and scanned the room
with the furtive expression of a man on the run.
He loped across the dance floor and knelt beside Rube.
"Are you—." Rube nodded. "Can you—help—?"
How could he have found someone
who had barely deplaned—unless—*unless*—
it was someone whose face was
known, like Melvin Belli, or the actor . . .

and listened intently to the sounds he blurted
underneath the fugal drumbeats.
Rube got up without a word. The two men walked

to a red column where the light was low—
but not low enough to subdue
the stranger's disturbed flailing arms. . . .
But who was the stranger?
Rube did not move. The others, as if bent
on the boys staying put, exchanged
sips from the spiked "punch" they guzzled out of
porcelain coconut shells, and asked to hear
once more about the explosion
and the gauze bandage on his hand.

There was a wall between him and the mystery.

The floodlights and the dust of stars.

The paw of the ocean on the shore.

ROLE PLAY

1. On location. Set off from real life by an artificial
world yet part of life—?

2. The set: a lovesick empire in the heat
during the long shoot in the Spanish hills.

3. The stillness of waiting is broken only
when a sunstruck actor, encased in his tin

shell of armor, clattered to the ground,
sweat oiling the skin from underneath the thin

film of Vaseline applied to simulate sweat.
The budget swelled like dropsy.

4. Excess without wisdom. And yet
the public loved to hear about the real

love that flared on the world's
stage between the long adored actress

(from the ingenue's "pre-erotic sentience")
and the upstart mercurial Welshman.

5. Love isn't a bad way to go when the cells of
the body politic are still

stunned by a regicide in which the victim
had no time to display

Cleopatra's uncommon courage . . . and fix
one serene final gaze on the reeling globe.

6. (Horace could not force the future
to listen when he warned: *wind*

shakes the tallest pine, lightning
strikes the highest tower . . .).

7. Why finish the film, why get out
of the characters whose passion,

mythic, wild, unbudgeted,
rivaled their own

when they could go on
falling forever in the

unsteady, giddy, delirious
gleam of that freedom?

8. They became the roles they played.
But like those lovers who came before

they fell prey to . . . magical thinking . . .
and thought: *if we ignore the world*

and make a new life in a far off place
it will . . . leave us alone.

9. The tabloids covered their every move:
and from here on in, whether spear-fishing

the Technicolor coral reefs off Puerto Vallarta
after Burton was done

with his whiskey-priest role in

Night of the Iguana

or taking each other on the hot white sand,
or whirling in the local cantinas, high

on atomic margueritas, (Cuervo
Gold, Cointreau, ice and lime) *nunc*

est bibendum, they could not shake the un-
easy feeling you get when you're being watched,

and your behavior, in ways you cannot
measure, is . . . : changed.

10. But *learning how to make the best of it
is the whole* . . . and there were

compensations; the small,
prelapsarian coastal town

was not a bad place to fall;
the streets smelled sweet after rains,

the noon sun shone through
the emerald green of iguanas;

and the smoked fish on sticks
hawked for centavos by peasant children

running barefoot up and down the beach
could not be beat: at any price.

(after Horace, Odes, Book I, 4 and 37)

DISTRACTED IN BEVERLY HILLS

A gambler, I'm not. I get distracted.
Something else always arrests my attention:
the way the players hold their cards,
the tension in the set of their faces;
or worse, ambient noise, the whirring
of a fan that fills the whole room.
I was a guest at a high stakes game.
The regulars were the legendary offspring
of Hollywood thises and thats:
half-god third generation Tarzans;
simulators of animal voices
cursed by the cartoon limits on language—
or of men who knew their way around money.
I had seen squalor and privilege
in a dizzying geography of cities
in a zigzag existence that kept any main drag
from dragging, but this—this was far,
far from the nowhere I always came back to—

If I didn't see repetition as *horror*,
I could set this before you plainly;
but this isn't about me.
It's about a town about which America
knows too much; craven for the hard facts
beyond life and care and dreams of elsewhere. . . .
Not to pass judgment: no one was
fully out of their teens; the war was
vociferous; everyone was scared—
not of the plague-death that has taken its place
in the lists of fears, but of death
by bomb, gun, grenade, or mine
in rice-paddies in a climate so humid
you'd forget to step lightly, or warily
every weary self-conscious step of the—way.
Was the perfect annihilation of thought
on those waterways and in those screens of reeds

an unknown, an unsuspected grace?

The pot mounted, a mound of bills and coins;
a watch; a ring; several traveler's checks . . . (mine . . .).
No one had pulled more than three of a kind
through the afternoon's eternal limbo;
impacted; frozen like Disney; waiting
for the genie—or whatever could release
its arrested spirit—. On the surface of it
everyone was having a good time.
I was; almost; or mostly—but the unease
that rarely left me was in high gear.
Neither animus or want of hard cash
made me lock horns with the boy my host
looked up to most on this planet:
the unflappable Mel Caesarian,
whose bangs and pudgy exterior concealed,
I'd been assured, a killer; a kid
so tough his low-key, subdued, yet steely manner
made Hell's Angels break out in goose pimples,
get back on their bikes with excuses
about having to be elsewhere. . . .
The room had heated up considerably by now.
I needed to be outside, as I often do
and started down the driveway,
long as the Main Streets of many small towns,
to lie on the depilated lawn
where overhead the house lights
of Beverly Hills combined
to eclipse the faint, domesticated stars.
Who cared if the haze was aura or flawed sight?
Any whiff of the infinite brings perspective.
I laughed out loud at my own . . . heaviness.
And brought the gardener out of the hedges,
brandishing a tined rake.
"It's all right," I said, "I'm with them."
"Oh," he said, "I thought you might be someone else."
I had said the right thing!
It was time to go back in.

I was ready to—PLAY CARDS!
There's a rhythm to shuffling that's almost
hypnotic; the cards make an infinitesimal
fluted whistle that accompanies the scud
over a hard surface; and the two
together, if you let yourself listen, are lethal
if what you want to get out of the game
is to win when loss, love's shadow, being infinite,
holds an altogether vaster vastness. Emptiness.

I'd been poker-faced before out of fear.
Now I feigned my non-expression to make
the others think I was thinking *real hard*,
about whether to stay in or go out,
when, feigning recklessness, I raised Mel's raise—
"Call," he said. I pushed my three of one suit
and two of another toward the center, *Real slow like*;
Caesarian spread out his hand. "Ten high."
Something was wrong, but I'd no idea what.
I forced myself to reach for the mound.
"Hey, what are you doing?" voices whined; chimed.
No one knew my name. I was no one to them.
"I don't think you understood," Caesarian said,
in the heralded hoarse, under-the-table voice.
"We were playing low card."
"Do you think I would have stayed
in and played out my full house
if I'd known? I was outside
when the game was called."
The clique's eyes clicked like shutters
as each sought each other out: if ONE of them had not
HEARD—the hand could be—ERASED;
that was clear from the look that Rick
was throwing me, a look suffused with fear, hope . . . ,
and something I could not identify. . . .
But everyone else had heard the dealer
call (mumble) "Low card." I did not want to give in
to the self-revulsion stirring within,
and replayed the moments that led up to this

catastrophe: I must have
wandered back in at the precise
moment when the dealer, finished with shuffling,
slaps the deck down and asks
if anyone wants to "cut."

II

THE MILLENNIUM HOTEL

They cut off beards, that's usual, assembled 45 Jews in the marketplace, led them to the slaughteryard, tortured, cut out tongues, wails heard all over the square.

ISAAC BABEL

The human race is never free from worry, and since the last judgment will take place in the street, it's obvious that in a hotel you won't have far to go. Let the trumpeting angels come, we hotel dwellers will be the first to get there.

LOUIS-FERDINAND CELINE

THE MILLENNIUM HOTEL

Prologue and Lament

for M.W.

I

Yearning scans the calendar
for the birthday of a loved one;
yet that January date is set against

sleet ticking on crusted snow-ice,
white wings
fluttering in eaves, white

shawls of smoke rising against
an off-white sky,
sky

which watches the larger urban settlements struggle.
What is there: other than weather?
Shifting

masses of particles.
A closet's dark depth plumbed in search of a forgotten
coat.

And every trivial errand remembers us
to be among the many
to be forced to see.

Grief—is friend to some.
Remember me
is what it repeats.

And that's enough—for an afterlife.
Heaven is just.
Opaque; imageless.

The scattered tribes ought to be
used to wandering by now—
living life like life

during the last days in a transit camp,
thin mattress in a roll at the foot of the bed,
and happily build

invisible temples
inside themselves . . .
which cannot come to ruin.

Silence is no less relentless.
Overcoming all.
But what is all?

2

Nothing Seasonal

The year is already a system of betrayals, disorder rife
in the cisterns of heaven: nothing overflows that does not
flood. The levees useless when the Mississippi fugues.

That's the story. No escape. Only wind rising now
in the outer reaches, high turbulent swirls,
stirring up the ashes on urns and the rims

of volcanoes, only wind, traveling, traveling,
having clocked enough mileage over time
to travel freely now, forever.

Only what is invisible knows the mercy
of shadow and light, as now shapes pass
through the third story window on far off

Broadway, the light varies its touch
with infinite . . . care? . . . above the peppermint
stripes of the art-deco diner's awning. Lights

change. Passersby hesitate and move on.
Journey through snowdrifts. Hoping there are still
provisions on supermarket shelves.

Hoping: you cannot live without some form of hope,
and the mind, the mind always makes the most out of the least,
like the prisoner of outer space who transforms a flesh and blood

robot into a real woman. Like children
freed of the fear of abandonment for an hour.
Time is cadenced, like the footstep.

There is nothing seasonal about this.
The real is slippery. But it is not so bad.
Ice on the fire escapes and window ledges.

Cars are on a long road to nowhere, ice-locked.
Ice—looks like it should last longer: the blob-
shapes on ledges take on degrees of hardness,

and darkness, ingrained, dark spots,
messy, chaotic, uneven, perplex the inner life of ice.
Why should it awaken surprise to see so many

bright, expressive faces moving through the iron air
and over the sulfurous drifts.
The cold's entrapments.

❧

Everything he needs is six blocks away
LUCINDA WILLIAMS

You can't live in New York and let minor irritations
get to you: I wish I had reached faster and
dug deeper—to help her?—or not to hear
her shriek—her miserable outburst—her
howl of abandonment—her authentic
theater of grunts and lurchings—.
Artaud would have cast her on the spot,
built a play around her unappeasability.
Do you think I am saying something like:
I couldn't have helped anyway; or only temporarily.
I could, at best, have offered her a Band-Aid.®
Where would the ones I saw proudly striding down
Broadway go if this isolate's chaos and disorder
were not "Six Blocks Away"—: songs
are like destiny: they pass
and pass; in waves, like love. And the couple
in that apartment where the blinds are raised
act like they're in love; she'll burst
into the room where one or the other
takes the interminable shift at the computer terminal
and hurl herself on his lap and hug him.

3

The Path

What would John Constable do faced with these
disappearing urban vectors and / or / if
interrupted in media stroke

on this frozen windblown corner
by a shrill, hysterical, and underdressed
woman—a human being—(for whose misery I am not

responsible) who walks away before I can
dig into my pants for the obligatory
quarter. (Why not more?)

Would he see her as part of the landscape or
an aberration?—an insult
to the lovely harbor stasis:

boats on ice, boats wrapped
in tarps, a stillness
broken only by the groan of wood

when wind and wave break
the rhythm the walkers create,
the women walking fast

enough to get their heartbeats up
but not too fast to miss
what the world wills them to

see: this whitish light as it ignites
the parapets . . .
There are souls worth saving!

I can hear Frederick Law Olmstead saying that.
Let them see each other, but at a distance.
There was no path before they burst out,

a man and a woman, in full stride, supple,
heels landing softly yet firmly,
the light creamy now, engorged.

The runners slip out of sight,
they move similarly, maybe
alone, they will dream of each other . . . —

while at the pier the familiar
pilings lift off like rockets,
the metal fences and warped,

waterlogged planks cut loose
from disused docks are listening;
and branches reach out, but only

slightly, since there is no wind
or what wind there is is scarcely measurable,
scarcely more than

air, air itself; but this
rough turquoise—coin toss between
teal and ultramarine—this stammering

delirium threatens
the flavescent leaves and the women
wearing monochromatic tights

while everything above the waist is so
rainbowed as to send
Joseph's weavers back to the loom.

It is the privilege of the living
to create a tone and rhythm that never will be again;
that defines their generation.

The chaos, as on the Corso, reflects selves found,
not lost, among the many.
The boats wrapped in tarps, chaste—

yet actively rocking on the swells,
as if their keepers had decreed
to let them maunder, unused, in their slips,

throughout the foreverness of the long
off season. Should we let the calendar
determine our lives?

Or was their anticipation of the cold
wind blowing in off the Hudson
prescient and just?

(My wife shaking out her auburn hair
and threatening to tighten
this abundant drift into a bun.)

We never get to any other place:
the chestnut-haired parapet,
the hush of the river,

the city in the clarity of winter light;
the sky like a blue window I could look through
endlessly forever,

as if it cared enough to dare me to stare
long enough to find out
how long, how far.

❧

But the pavements of upper Broadway
and Greenwich Avenue were not put there
for prolonged metaphysical speculation;

nor are the circumstances in which I find myself
there, en route to meet a commitment, aware
that closer study of the layout of the street

would cause me to be late: a public school
playground reconciles the row of beleaguered
tenements with the happiness of two-story brownstones.

4

Stormwatch

For a week or so, between this new year
and the old, every time I spoke

of one parent or another dying,
I thought it is

as if people in their forties
are at that point on the conveyor belt

of their allotted time on earth,
(—in that time of dying—)

that they must witness their parents exit—step
off—the far end.

Death—is the paragon of patience.
It is not intelligent. It holds—all the cards.

It knows where matters of time are concerned
there it must triumph. Hollow victory.

No two people take it in the same way.
Life is an apprenticeship in mourning.

Light keeps the presentation dramatic:
it heightens the value of shade.

All that work to forge the link between sex
and death. Foreplay is like what a given

life was like. The end doesn't give a damn
about the steps which led up to the door.

The indelible individual
footprint. Death has read our Constitution:

and all prisoners of the temporal chain
are equal in the sightless eyes of death.

᪥

Primordial antidote:
salt strewn on a pavement.

And because I live here I must
be part of the storm watch.

One winter I noticed that the soot-blackened
snow crusts and the ash-flecked lava-
crusts on the island of Hawaii

felt the same to walk
                    over, on, in,
making a distinct impression, as if incised
            every time you put your foot down, took

another step in the same no-direction,
leaving footsteps like polygraphs: height
and weight, tendencies, *being*, ineradicably

written on the blankness; and what luck
that weather and quakes, in sudden
catastrophic jumps, destroyed

the signs, the evidence, clues, and proof—
inviolable seismograph.

When a psychoanalyst friend with whom
I often converse was firm that I must
promise not to forget the—unexamined—

reasons people yearn
for *closure* and to beware
theories about memories you can't remember

I nearly fell
headlong off the stationary bicycle,
because other people's need for closure,

irresolute resolution

has *ruined my life*

—while the question and the mystery stand
gaping, open, torn, maligned, poked at . . .

BADGERED

Item: now it's begun, the well-advertised storm
the assault on stasis and order
minus the devastation of the coast-

line, the wave-roar under
the pick-up-stick houses on the shore,
undercutting anything
on stilts.

The storm: and now a woman out the window at dawn
drags a heavy suitcase alone: where is she going?

Where is her frenzy of desire leading her?

I notice, even as the infinite trucks pour in,
old clocks for sale in the display window of
an unnamable store (neither junk shop

nor antique) a place whose mission
in life is torn between passion and commerce:

the immediate and the need to cull a profit.

(Who knows how it stays alive in the waning?)

It's far and near, intimate and infinite,

sound of wind in a monochromatic world
given a home—with the doors open and you
shivering in the back meadow overgrown with snow.

But is it far from
where either of us is positioned—
in life and death—(riding the storm's eye?).

Positioned.

My friend, a native of Montpelier,
goes home for Christmas to visit Mom,
stays pinned to
CNN for storm warnings,
(as if it were as far off as the desert

war

and the apocalyptic crawl of armored vehicles, this

— "Nor'Easter of 94" —

And it is of use after all to see what happens over time and a
good idea to be alive to mark the (barely perceptible) changes:

    zigzag on sofa and rug; chairs
    turned around, away
    from the wilding views,
    the pursuant avenues,
    the abrupt eruption
    (after living here
    for many—years—)
    of shows for the eager voyeurs,

—a man I thought I might have been,
and fail at, and am not—

       I looked up to see a couple
making love. I did not become
           absorbed in what I saw.

5

The Millenium

I was thinking about you moments before I learned of your mother's death, and thinking about you—your situation—during the weekend I spent alone with Sam in room 1812 at The Millenium Hotel in lower Manhattan.

And everywhere that day I looked for buildings that were saturated in time, whose weathered brick, sandstone, or iron, was what gave it charm, in a way—character: like a dappled wall in Paris where a down and out street musician is roused to play a few bars on the clarinet, hopelessness itself is lost, and the mournful protagonist, who lifted him off the ground, cracks a smile at his renewed vigor and soon returns to composing again and signing her name instead of her (dead) husband's to her compositions. Grief surrounds the edges of everything with shadows.

Why did she survive?
Why are her husband and daughter no longer alive?

Alive. Popcorn, crackling.
The light no more toward her grief than yours.

Love: a matter of right and right.
She: "Why do you mourn?" Friend: "Because you don't."

Scraping knuckles along rough brick wall:
the bleeding hurts less than the other pain.

These footsteps on the stairs can't belong to the robber
she just saw moving quickly over the cobblestones below.

She longs to be alone in the dark that encumbers no one.
In the pool with shadows that do nothing more than change.

Everyone knows more of the future than he or she will admit.
Never is easier than will be.

As before you wanted to be more and more in water.

Every morning, when I step into the shower, I feel
high, as if each dawn I'd been reborn.
And each day I were being granted a fresh start.
And rather than being burdened with habits to break
so as to not take that which is a gift
for granted, I had no routine, no skin . . .

Gone the borderline between night and day.

Uneasy Solutions

After the dreams of water began I found a way
to be in the maelstrom with my eyes open
in the replica of dusk that grew
when, locking the bathroom door
I switched the light off, the shower—on.
For as long as the water poured
I was not who I was taken for.
The drops beat against the shell, tore
the armor I had grown in my state of unknowing
as I slithered to the floor.
The indignant stood on the other side
and cried out *you'll use up all the hot
water,* as if I had anything to do
with the *you* they were talking to.

*Why The Millenium? It's really a hotel for business people who don't care if
they're islanded, cut off from the world. Why not, talking upscale, The Plaza,
or, talking downscale, The Excelsior? Something with class, charm, history,
or at least . . . location?*

It's the only hotel I could find on no notice to escape to with a pool
and circuitous skies, reviving to impossible

blue-gray-gold,
through which the reddish brick can be itself again . . .

It never stops being odd
being snowed in
in a big city.

What would I not give for a working fireplace . . .

But if home were truly home I would not have
holed up at this hotel for the duration. . . .
The Financial District's stark iron immensity

is made human by Sam, for whom a plastic
stopwatch, perfect in its uselessness, brings
joy . . . and Tic Tacs and Trident . . . mean so much.

Only what we turn to changes, only where our
longing longs to dwell. . . .

                              ❦

*This made the moment more intense but it was not as if you wanted
it this way, you would have preferred a lighter time.*

(Lighter?)

I didn't know it then but the time was
already hurtling in my direction
when I would only be at ease, free of
pain that is, in water—if I lay still.
They say it's normal: painlessness
when you're free of gravity.

No one else in The Millenium was at poolside . . . but I found it
hard, even as I dove to gather Sam's "X-Men,"
Wolverine, Cyclops, and Gambit
with his phosphorescent card
to keep my eyes off the shape-shifting shadows,

the dark patches spreading from the edges,
and with them a procession of thoughts
that looked backward
to my dead father and forward to when Sam
would outgrow these dalliances with his Dad, he
would be in my place and I—nowhere—

I knew my father best in water;
only in water would he go along
with my antics; and I loved it when he held me
half in half out, afloat in time-
lessness. And now as
Sam's piping, insistent cries
of "Play" and "Hold me" filled the echoing room—
but joy and sadness were joined in one
motion, and the well-lit ripples streamed
and swirled on the glass around us
and I thought, "Stay illusion." . . .
Lights multiplied,
mirror simulations of ice,
ripples in the pool like northern lights
riddled with glitter
and planes arrowing down.

❦

Rain of Arrows at the "Dawn" of Memory

If a cavern yawns between the necessary and the good,
is it wider or deeper than the immense
distance between solitude and—loneliness?

Is it "greater than" the immeasurable
number of feet
that kept that window from jamming

against the adjacent L-shaped brick
that kept direct sun down
in the bedroom I shared with my mother

in our spare apartment only four floors
above the mirror-lined alcove
where her parents—

"one through blood and one through marriage—"
held colloquies on the correct way
to shovel food?

With my dime store quiver strapped to my back,
I savored
a moment alone

and stood, ten stories high, gazing out
this window over the indefinite;
the courtyard, alley, or street.

The arrows rattled: they lusted
for release, and to bridge
the emptiness between the window and the wall.

After endless practice
on hard, receptive surfaces
like our *boulevardier* wallpaper

sprinkled with innocent passersby
armed with umbrellas and beards,
why shouldn't I have hope?

When my aim was true the arrows stuck
until the air leaked out with a sigh,
a gratifying—*pop*—

like lips coming apart reluctantly
after a kiss—as suction subsided.
And now my arrow soared

for an instant before
it bounced off the rebarbative brick
and plunged down

the narrow shaft.
Undaunted, I set the second arrow
in its groove; drew the bow-string tighter;

squinted; took sharper aim.
Same result.
My heart galloped off so fast its crack

stunt rider landed on his back.
I knew the side effects of practical solutions:
that attaching a string behind the feather

would allow me to reel in the arrow
but also distress
its trajectory on the way down.

There was no reason on earth
why the arrows shouldn't . . . stick. . . .
But they were not "on earth."

The abyss was nothing—compared to the hollowness.
Then, out of nowhere, my expectations shifted,
and I was free to lose myself again

in the arrows' soundless arabesques.
When my quiver was empty,
I threw the bow out the window.

6

Around this time you began making transcontinental flights alone.

I lived in air, emptier than emptiness
each breath of wind a wound.

And every time, and there were so many,
the view was occluded by clouds

all went quiet in the cabin.

Were the others holding their breath?

I was immersed in a fog of unknowing;

mystified:

—how could the pilot fly calmly
through what he could not see?—

                              Nothing was less
natural.

I trusted pilots, but the machine sounded
ill: whining, grasping, groaning; vibrating,
according to my calculations, too
violently for its own frame.

And when this transitorily functioning depressed object
kept in the jet stream through the grace of care-
ful, skilled technicians—

like a gloomy, doom-ridden character,
all the time fighting off
the time-bomb of self-destruction locked within—

finally reverted to what it had always been,

that rivet would pop.

The tailspin would begin.

❧

It's riskier at lower altitudes.

I love machines, but I don't trust them.

It's predictable, the way they wear out.

And break down in the desert with no one around
except men who've eased themselves down
between camels' humps.

7

After the Storm

In my dream last night I wanted to return to the "Heights,"
the small Midwestern town where I learned
to free my soul from the clutches of others as I wandered
the desolate flat unbroken blank terrain no one
thinks to   praise   or compare to mountain, desert, or sea . . . ,
but what can a child do alone amid such extremes
other than fall, scorch, or drown,
whereas in the prairie you can wander without fear
of lion, scorpion, or shark,
though man-of-war would be more akin to a child's nightmare,
this child's anyway, since I'll never
unremember how, after a night of feverish sleep
in which every object in the room took on
shapes familiar yet alien—

the squall battering the Florida coast with its rapine,
shaking the towering palm trees free
of the hirsute, weighty, unattainable
treasures I could not will to fall or crack
open when I hurled them against a wall;
I found a string of bloated, purplish, boneless
bodies strewn on the sands I wouldn't dare
touch no matter how dead they looked to be but had to poke (and
poke) with a long stick or small log,
because deep down I knew they were only
feigning death, resting up after the whirlwind, waiting,
as mariners wait for wind, or a long
wave to sweep them back
into their element, where they belong.

8

"And What If It Had Been His Last Wish . . ."

Whenever we hit our no-frills hotel anywhere in the warm
my father would issue his well-intentioned command:

"Go for a dip in the pool, and you'll feel brand new."
It was always a rainy windy night when we arrived.

The illuminated aquamarine of the painted pools,
tormented by heavy drops that burst like grapes,

splattered with parachutes that never opened,
made me hesitate and incited him to repeat

the recipe for renewal—this time with strain.
(Why was I so stubborn? Was I really his son?)

"I'm not paying for you to stay alone in a room,"
he'd throw in hoarsely, by now beyond

exasperation, as if it had been my idea
to zero in on this overcrowded temperate zone.

That *why do I waste time talking to you* tone
grew, or dwindled, over a chunk

of the century to a clipped, bare-bones,
"suit yourself, ok, Mark. . . ."

I knew he'd pour out his stock of pejoratives,
square, fidget (always checking to see if your

glasses are on), worrier, your mother's son,
when I stated quietly (*what, I can't hear you,*

speak up man!) that my lover and I would refrain
from going skinny dipping off the prow of the small

craft he lived on from dawn to dusk that last decade
when he cut the engines in a quiet cove, dropped

anchor, and busied himself unbelievably
with the tasks that came with the role of Captain,

with tackle, ladders, ice-chests, radio signals,
and slitting open half-frozen squid for bait.

"What are you waiting for? You both must be
burning, and—look around—no one can see."

He of course didn't count; he could spray his gaze
over my lover's lithe, lanky frame as she crossed

the deck with quick, graceful steps before diving in,
then help her up the ladder with—who could doubt it?—

clinical detachment: he'd seen more naked women than. . . .
And it was retro to be shy about the body.

Every word he never uttered but conveyed
through his super-casual-sea-salt-liberal

open-minded-quasi . . . was probably true.
Or at least half-true. Invisible beams angled in

to scald our skin and blind us via glare of sun
on water. As for being "fixed up with an ice-

cold Heineken" it had to worsen
the steady throbbing in my temples,

the relentless tightening.
Dying for a dip, I would not fall for it.

And my father's wish? It may not have been
wrong. But it wasn't his right.

9

The Stewardess

It was you and your father off the Mazatlan coast.
The bare room opened onto the gulf.

The tiles glittered like the scales of a mackerel.

You spotted her in the lobby,
checking in.

You passed her in the corridor.
Taut body, short-cropped hair.

She was young, perhaps not yet out
of her teens. But old enough

(whatever that means) to be a
stewardess for Mexicana Airlines.

And young enough to take you for
beyond your years.

I don't remember how I got into her room . . . ,
my ruse was some

                    "wonderful story
in Playboy" you "wanted to share with her."

She'd never seen it before.
And was eager to hear

you read it to her
and asked to know again the name

of the magazine. When the page fell
open to the touched-up nude

her expression remained the same.
By then you were getting hot.

Did you want to kiss her neck?
She didn't seem to mind.

*She was a kid like you only she lived
in the Real World.*

Real *Third* World.
Her robe was of a cotton so light.

And what would she be doing
with underwear on in her own room?

10

The Heights

How not to be seduced by the new?
The glittering simulacra.

High above it all in The Millenium
amid deceptive reflections: weightless mirrorings . . .
Why go to so much trouble in this viewless world,
where block facades outrace the Gothic, where the flat
vertical and horizontal grid
rubs out the reliquary, the ornate,
the greening eaves sea birds squeeze into in the storm,
the ornamental nymphs—deemed
useless— . . .

("obsolete" as Rod Serling said
whenever I found myself in earshot
of this New Year's Eve Twilight Zone Marathon . . .)

In a frozen world we rely
more than ever on the eye.

The four women in relief—
were they once angels?—
one prayerful, one sly, one soliciting,
one watching the others: is the day
when they would be simulated, like screen
dinosaurs, on its way, or already here
in the World Financial Center's indoor winter,
its lifeless, perfect arraignment;
like a little boy's maddened dreams of fighting
endless victories without harm,
over no one, everything, nothing . . .

If it's time to run it's not time
to run away: light-time brought together in one
swift, unstinting beam . . .

❧

One day: it comes: the answer!
And you are not in.

❧

The news is rife with information
about the cold: not one word about
the light: the blaze on the Hudson

answering . . . :

the golden disregard . . . in which all
is held . . . the luminous ice over
which we walk, traceless, found . . .
scattering snow's cocaine
in the emptiness of the Financial District
this frozen Sunday . . .

❧

The temptation of the heights.
Suddenly you look up and for an instant
you are sure you are sure
to be crushed . . . the vertical
at the base of these glass towers, tilts
forward, just as Caravaggio's figures
appear to leap, 3-D like, out of the canvases
which imprison them.

❧

What money and power have failed
to cover over, Trump Tower
and The Millenium Hotel will always fail
to bury in their arc of rising
terror: the composite
poverty of poverty, the impacted
rage carved in the genes, of those who know

only what they do not have.
Room Freshener can't undo
millennia of sorrow . . .

                               or the emptiness that kills

that lives with its finger on a hair-
trigger pistol . . .

Life is not this way; only death:
its sentries, henchmen, and messengers.

The news is sanguine. Why is there
no news of it?

                Yes, the desperation
of the poor is heightened too . . . in the city in winter . . .
but without this ice and light would the eye seek out,
at an uncertain height, the four stone women, once
angels perhaps, on this heavenly balcony?

II

1812

This young man you call 'Bonaparte' . . .
JOSEPH JOUBERT

Why were we granted room 1812 on an empty Sunday in frozen January,
and why did our view from this most cold modern and angular of places
include so much of the old world, Trinity Church and its small, dignified
graveyard?

Jury Duty

Walking here last May on my lunch break from the law
the light hit the time-darkened, turbulent stones
with such tender, fierce, erotic force,
like a match struck in a cave
I ground to a halt
and wanted to rub my skin
in, on, against, within . . . , but rested, restlessly,
content with the palm of my left
hand on the roughy granite and,
lightly, both cheeks . . . ,
and would have lingered
had not my citizen-reminder-beeper begun
its *this is not the time, this is not the place*
routine, as if this confluence could happen any day,
and our species were not endangered by the daily
catastrophe of delay . . . ;

and allowed myself to wonder
if when I am no longer around
to walk these underestimated streets
the world would be worse off
without me here to love it.

❦

I looked out the window and indulged in the image of another failed "final solution," another "invincible" army laid low, by the same unpredictable factor that brought us to this place; weather; the snow continuing beyond what the greatest tacticians could have predicted, as if a law of averages were ever truly useful in the short run. There are no true odds unless you factor in time.

♣

GOOD QUESTION

There is no losing when you're meant to win.
But how and when do we know which side destiny's on?

The gods like underdogs. To keep
the betting high in the casinos of heaven.

What the gods want: another throw of the dice.
(Is this what it is to be more than human?)

Take away the dimension of time in gambling
and the odds are less in favor of the house.

Then why, knowing loss is temporary,
knowing they have to win

over time, are they so vicious
at play in their precious casinos?

—Or is there a chance they don't know
knowledge is not enough?, that what is

immeasurable means more
(and is in danger, every day,

of falling away) than a horde
of cashed-in chips.

❧

When you reach bottom you're in a clean place.

Stepping out of icy air to worm through underworld tubing, you descend shimmering elevators and stairs and reach the tree-lined colonnade, the world of a landscape architect whose luxury it was to work without "nature's interfering mess and chaos." Music piped in from invisible speakers, the sound of Muzak, the spare, barely modulated melodic line of yesterday's "new sound."

Which all of Soho flocked to Town Hall to hear.

The majority, who turned up in white painter's pants, are turning thirty and either committing themselves to art for life or reverting to type, returning to the World of Their Parents, ranging from suburbs where life is a dream, to small towns and dingy cities they'd lived to escape, like Lucien de Rubempré—whom Balzac imported from the provinces so he could lose his illusions—and the gamblers in *La Peau de Chagrin* who thought they could clamber up to heaven without a ladder. And others whose names, fictional or real, you're free to fill in.

❧

When does the pride in fashioning things unreal begin, or begin to yield? Why was the finest Chinese restaurant I have ever eaten in in Manhattan situated in this plant-infested underworld, where no ray of sun will ever pierce the kaleidoscopic fishtank where no fish I'd ever laid eyes on before fanned their fins? It was the first time Sam could be induced to eat more than sesame noodles ("not spicy"), to lament the smallness and scarcity of spare ribs per portion (four, at the cost of more than a dollar per, and with four orders of these tidbits you can see where this meal was heading . . .) and to submit to a tasting of the soup (in its exquisitely small and detailed bowl) and asking for more, more everything, more cashew-sized chicken nuggets on a skewer . . . —when I had to pull the plug: these microscopic dishes were costing more than our manic-delirious room service order of

55

The Millenium Hotel	
hamburger	$12.68
caesar salad	$11.25
coke	$5.37
coffee	$7.57
gratuity	$15.00
TOTAL	$51.87

Thank You! ☺

My mother was shocked at these expenditures even while I patiently shouted that this one night at The Millenium was our winter's luxury, escape, and splurge.

So what's wrong with The Plaza . . . a place with some class, some charm?

No pool.

12

Our beautiful mothers! Death isn't the worst of it:
death-in-life is worse and if your mother really lived

that—is blessedness. (Maybe a certain lightness
can be obtained, without loss of truth . . .)

Now technos outreaches the spirit's grasp of what it all means,
our mothers everywhere mesmerize their remaining hours,

eyes pinned to anxious-making CNN.
My mother heralds storms days before they reach me here,

a thousand miles from where she schools herself on the occluded
itinerary of the future. And she's not alone:

the mother of the woman in *Blue* sits fixed before her screen in Paris,
and could care less about the weather: she watches

elderly daredevils, ropes attached
to their horsecollars, jump from rooftops

to mirages of swimming pools below.
Slow motion close-ups repeat the scene.

13

Walker's Pond

And to think I almost held back because the water was too cold!
Beyond the messy weed strewn shallows
the water seals itself at my feet.
Pockets of cold, pockets of warm.
When I rise to draw another breath
a jet goes by, almost diaphanous, like a cloud.
Effortlessly my stroke quickens.
Trees reel; horizons widen and multiply.
I wouldn't have guessed there were witnesses
had not the glint of cliffside binoculars
blunted my ecstasy.
Now I go down deeper and stay below
for as long as my breath holds out.
It takes effort to stay below without straining:

as when the plane, descending in the dead
of night, comes to where the lights from towns and cities
blink like auras through the clouds
which only then seemed lit from within,
self-generating, not charged with energy from generators;
and these hazy lights, these auras, these mirages,
which first appeared as horizons,
moved throughout the body of the night;
and when they disappeared and the gray cotton was stuffed
into my eyes and ears and I could not breathe
the plane touched down, jerked, skidded, tilted,
and leveled off . . . , all a question
of when and where to plunge in, when
to resist, stand by: wait.

14

Semaphore

Don't ask me what
I'm getting at.
What is there to get
at, where
is there to go. Space,
a grid of limits,
cartographer's heaven.

Heaven is what does not
go on in the physical
world. There is no
Bergen-Belsen in heaven.
Jews are put away,
made a breed apart,
for praying to an invisible,

and therefore invincible,
God.
His near absence.
Crossroads, not crosses.
The anxious instant.
They are reviled
for not demanding proof,

that God have a body. There are good
reasons for Jew
hating: look at
Fyodor Ivan Dostoyevsky Karamazov
for whom the obscene mute,
suffering of children was proof
God does not exist.

Justice does not come in a box
with Creation.
Who said the violence

that brought us to this place
was any less volcanic
than what it is?
It wasn't the Nazis

but the ones who wanted
answers
who herded your mom and dad
through the gates of Bergen-Belsen.
The problem
was never that the best
lacked conviction but that

they needed it to override uncertainty
and live as if life was not pure
chance or a mad, wild game of charades
in the dangerously volatile
hands of shape-shifting maniacs.

*An artist with murderer's hands; that was the ticket,
the hieroglyphic of the times.*

Shelley grasped this
riding Venetian shores at dusk
beside his Mephistophelean sidekick
whose keen eye at billiards and the physics
of bank shots helped clue him in
that beyond religion lay the gift
of chance.

It's why diaspora ought to signify
semaphore, open door,
all who wander
and come to be here, here,
in the fullness of nowhere;
to be in
unyielding

chaos emptying
like the earthquakes percolating

all the time on the big
island—inviolable
seismograph.

⚘

The train platform at night in Indian Hill.
The approaching headlight like a liquid lens—

all I could see of the train—
like pure spirit moving through space.

The heat coming off it as the whistle shrills.
The lights going out in the houses.

The sky turning from charcoal to pitch-black.
The train so far away, then near.

Three teenage girls, each with braces and acne,
ecstatically giggling on the metal plates between the cars.

⚘

To love—the wholeness
of unknowing—which is not to say not
to crave order in the day to day,
the repetition without which
children cry out that they cannot sleep
under strange sheets
because they aren't "used to it,"
because—here's the order of events at home—
and that's what they must do
to let their hands fall
open.

⚘

Uncertainty: gambler's paradise, groundless ground.

♧

Only unsaying is endless.

♧

She entered the blizzard and disappeared.

Do you wonder why your mother's
natural if excruciating death
has provoked this barrage of questions? Because a pall
of silence has fallen
over . . .

You must think twice
when you come
face to face with evil
because it's not all right.

♧

Thursday the 13th,
mourning morning,
the skies of 9:45
shrouded in dawn's
ratty overcoat,
the heights with-
drawing, light-
ning quick,
beam of light-time,
death's
termite
messengers,
morning sirens
en route to rescue
unless it is too
late, another
rooftop jumper—
whom no mother-goddess
outfitted at the last

second with wings
like Aesacus:
vein-slitters
prone to procreate
death at dusk—

No vein no gain
of entrance to
Terminus Junction,
resurrected stop
on once defunct
Orient Express—

❧

Time remembers what it didn't do on a given
day, like hold on to the passing
hour, cloud—

The heights don't warm to us, they warn us—
faltering humility,

as if when, walking Madison in the blaze
life seems endless

light breaking in on these perilous yet high-
ly colorful streets, sandstone and brick
giving back the ripeness they have gathered
over time.

The crowded death camps of air and earth

     freed of deluded hope—

     your eyes never glazed over
     from the piped-in dreams
     first of the world's
     last wings.

Yesterday's snow-banks, today's ice

for which I did not ready my twain
eyes and feet.

Premonitory stars—

Glimmer
of electric bulbs
rimming these wire branches.
Like premonitions, but of what
I cannot say.

♣

We are seduced too easily by illusory orders, definitions of what consti-
tutes sense.

Sense—bursts apart. What role does our anticipation of the great freeze
have on the weather?

The blizzard gives the question leave to answer.

The heights whirl themselves
ferociously upward.

Repercussions

We emerged starry-eyed from the ophthalmologist's office.
And now it was too late for the four o'clock
showing of Schindler's List, we'd earned
the reward of a movie, and the baby-sitter
we'd hired to ensure
this—freedom—was already whisking Sam to the 72nd St.
McDonald's, Madelaine had brought the C
section of the *Times*, but who
could read the time any other possible

films were showing? Who after an eye-exam
can consider more prolonged immersion in the dark
with your attention at every instant directed,

your mind—controlled—without eating something first,
which broached (though hunger wants to say *poached*)
the question of which way to turn
on Columbus. The time was right
for a movie I only half-wanted to see
(it would begin at 5:23) and a Sushi

Bar swam toward us through the mist:
perfect! Except that in
looking up at the blazing
signs and reticulate bulb-studded branches,
while balancing the simultaneous
hungers for sustenance and escape,
gravity had not forgotten me; and that while my back
was turned the snow-crust had undergone
a metamorphosis and now claimed

a harder, colder, slicker substance: called ice.
The salt-gnawed soles of my Timberlanes
gripped nothing.
And I went down.
It wasn't the worst of falls, quick and smooth,
like a last second slide which leaves the catcher
wishing he'd never heard the phrase *routine
play*; it was nothing like going down
on the black ice on the back road in Cabot;

nothing like the root-clusters of Riverside Park
that sent my tired shell hurtling headlong into gash and crises;
dirt, shit, and stone burrowing deep inside my left knee . . . ;
nothing like my descent when, undone by an underlayer of mud,
my feet, in smooth-soled shoes, gave way,
and I would have hurtled headlong toward the roaring
clefts of the waterfall had I not landed on a torn
stump that gashed my back and held
when I crooked my elbow around it;

nothing like the worst of these disasters
that owed nothing at all to weather,
when in that school for juvenile delinquents

I fell into a hole and jammed my thigh
to where the skin and muscle
pushed to bone like an enormous C.
And no one else had fallen.
And it was the only way to get to the showers.
And when the handsome nurse asked me to call home

I wanted to say, If I had a home
what was I doing here, dragging my life
behind me. I wasn't an orphan.

15

Night Thoughts

When I brood on Germany in the night
No hope for sleep. I know I'll lie
Awake with my eyes wide open while
Tears scald my cheeks.

The years are a blur of past and future:
A good twelve of them have passed since I last
Laid eyes on my mother—which may be why
I'm in such a frenzy to see her.

And I am desperate with desire.
I am under the old mutter's spell.
She circles my mind like a ring of fire.
I hope to god she is alive and well.

She loves me to pieces, the old woman,
And when in her letters her script breaks down,
I know she's shaken to her depths, I know
When the mother in her's shocked by her role.

My mother never leaves my mental space
Free of time past, the twelve long years,
Twelve!—that vanished without a trace
Since our last satisfying hug and kiss.

Don't worry about Germany: it's the picture
Of health. It will outlast us. All and all.
I'll know its borders again by the flare
Of its barbarous oaks and lime-trees' salute.

I wouldn't waste a moment thinking on
Germany were it not for my mother . . . ;
Fatherland-is-forever; but the old
Woman, being mortal, may soon grow . . . cold.

Since I left the country death has taken
Many I loved. And now the unbreathing
Impinge too much upon my sympathy.
Numbering the dead does me in.

And yet I feel compelled to count and each
Body added to the tally has a say
In how my mourning grows: hordes of corpses
Crush my chest. What—relief—when they . . . give way.

Praise the lord. And the lighter light of France
That through this window breaks as my wife, well-
Tempered, radiant as dawn, dispels
My German burden with her lovely smile.

after Heinrich Heine

16

Succulents subjected—

swimming in the yet unwritten language of dusk
to dust

This is what the snow is not:
an omen, good, bad, or

      why break down,
      we who
      follow you—

only fools (like us) take
snowfall as a sign
of higher order when each
flake is chaos
incarnate.

(Incarnadine only
after my last
fall.)

Chaos is worth praying for.

Your fate comes off your face one
particle at a time.

The multitudinous small
changes in every
      fate
is all we can know so partially
fate to fate
where the lies, the false eyes

of witnesses create
the losses we betray

What are we to make of our
passage, the enforced brevity
of our fate

They had to pry the queen of hearts
from the murdered card reader's fist.

The park, which keeps alive its dream of being
a wilderness again for good
                    reason.

17

How far can we take chance, can chance take us?

৵

Of chaos and the weather,
of what is, not what is not,
recurrences, recrudescences,
the ice's deceptions,
uncertain reflections,
its persistence on the pavement so long
after the skies have cleared
(their hard enamel baked in what   kiln?)
the trudge and groan of human . . . moan . . .

"The bow . . . can I . . . touch it?"

eking out a . . .

Children in another world . . .
dragging sleds without gravity . . .
toward the park's hillocks . . .

ignorant of its "dangers" . . .

৵

Who said anything about being nervous?

It's true I find it difficult to breathe this week but the hapless passersby
I've surprised on streetcorners to question them about the condition of
their lungs all confirm (in spite of yesterday's flagrant sun) that while
they themselves might not be suffering that they have, this winter, suf-
fered, or know of others who have suffered, and that I should not be
deceived by the painfully brilliant light or apparent clarity of the sky
because the air is packed with chemicals and the snowbank's saturated
with poisonous gases which, just because we can't see them being emit-
ted doesn't mean they aren't penetrant, and besides—it's damp.

＊

Passing the Claremont Stables gives me leave to pause: for less than one session with an analyst, for only a dollar a minute, I can ride in circles in a ring and not think twice about my horse sliding on ice.

But why should I pay to go nowhere
when I'm already on my way
        somewhere?
here, here—

            in history

＊

Of course I didn't know when I set out,
in rabid need of ink, around the block,
that the graying Indian stationer
who mans his station dawn to dusk

and claims to be *out of black right now*
I have blue-black and blue
come back in an hour
and I'll have it for you

would add "I hope this storm doesn't . . . come . . .
people suffer . . . a winter like this . . ."
—waves his arms—
"MEANS THE END OF THE WORLD"

＊

From CNN to MTV—

(Butthead: "Tornadoes are cool."
Beavis: "Yeah. They can suck your heart out of your chest."
Butthead: "Maybe the world's coming to an end."
Beavis: "Yeah. The end of the world. That would be cool.")

72

The fifteenth nor'easter of this unreal winter
set to return at any hour, my breathing
shallow and difficult from God   knows what
alignment of astrological signs

chemicals in the air
exhaust fumes fermenting in ruined snowbanks
and good old cold and damp
which does not love our lungs

but if Beavis and Butthead can, insouciant,
—heads bowed low, hair blown back—
bicycle into a tornado
(which is why, I suppose, the streets

of the cartoon town are deserted)
the citizens already   underground—
and meet two babes who intercept
them outside their wind-rocked trailer

and say "Since we're going to die
maybe you guys could be our last date"
surely I   can cope
and promise when spring comes

to do better with regard to the world:
to scour the neglected streets
whose pavements have lain so long
under siege of snow and ice,

whose concrete nerves are raw
from shovels coming at them,
jarring the hazardous surface.

✧

You'd think I could step
into the Cafe Brigitte
for a quick fricassee
at the counter

and an unfancy taste of France,
without encountering
a police "**Barricade At Saint Vincent's**"
which I cannot pass by

without asking a cop,
who has strayed toward the margins
"What happened?"
"Three People Shot On Brooklyn Bridge"

"Why did they bring them here?"
"This is where they brought them."
THREE . . . Hasidim . . . In retaliation
for the "**Mass Murder In The Mosque**".

✧

The little boy and I walk across the campus in the battering wind that
tossed umbrellas and sent less nimble-footed citizens awkwardly down
steps, clutching emptiness for balance; but in spite of blasts from the
north and the ice-patches we still   paused   when ambushed by the

MOON

in the plush blue-black
in the enamel-hard, purplish, nocturnal

SKY

balanced between the schools
of business, law, philosophy, and art

18

(Pause.)

Your condition is yours.
But it does not belong to you.

Exile: blessed contagion.

Her father couldn't sleep for three years after her mother died.

When you have lost everyone and everything,
husband, children, land, you can still exercise
one freedom: the freedom to howl, and lament.

Take heart: you're learning to see in the dark.
To be: in the interstitial absence.

The gap. The gulf. And each provisional bridge is portable.
Nothing is hidden in the darkest darks, the absolute black
death initiates . . .

❧

The window vibrating slightly in its frame through no force of wind.

Speculum mirror of the sky intact, virginal (vaginal and verging),
through all its many lives. The same sigh the sky lives to breathe.

The view like details of a Dutch interior: domestic trifles, heightened
brick, windows like foggy portals into lives you never see, but know
someone is there, behind the curtains, just as when mist covers the
mountain and you take heart and wait with the hope

it will reappear.

You say nothing of yourself.

Because too much has happened and to lie down now for half an hour as
the sky catches its breath and pent-up clouds race beyond thought of any

finish line and some bedraggled plants put up a good fight below the red
shades and a pair of sheeted windows practice the zen of blankness, koan
of casting off the bridles of

hope and despair,
                    and delusion, and the bare
torsos in Vanity Fair . . .

like the bubbles they blow
below the hostile statue's bronze confusion
and draw the peacock out
from the fixed domain
of the herb garden to actually

stand up on the plaque . . .

The cries of children rise and waft in endless—

It will never be this day again.
That isn't fun to think about.

Why should it be fun? The same Thursday
in May will return but the clouds

won't be the same, the sky's Rorschach will be
other, as will the children blowing bubbles

under the monster's malevolent claw.
Or in his shadow.

I'll give you odds the indigo necked
(are they all?) peacock will be back

wandering the herb garden he so
rarely strays from.

Joseph Joubert puzzled the question of repetition
while his carriage paused between inns;

(striking Alpine views, the horses drained from laboring in these
higher altitudes,
                the women looking for an appropriate
place to raise their skirts
                        within skirts
and pee
        with a little privacy,

(but where, when cliffs on either side
of slender road fall sheer
                    and forever . . . ?)

They manage. Women always do.

And the men don't care.
They'll piss anywhere.

His sentence breaks off there
(always, everywhere)

He is drawn to what he'll never know.

And hope these climes—are hospitable
        to good wines

19

March

The heat of the sun
crazes the stunned
ravines. For the new
season as for the farm

girl trying not to spill
a drop of water from
the brimful pail,
chores are endless.

Sluggish, anemic, the old snow
holds on yet wastes away,
shot through with blue
twig-like veins.

In the barn all is warm,
breathing, snorting,
steaming, frothing.
Tines of pitchforks gleam.

Days and nights become one
in weather, eaves pour out
buckets of water at noon,
culverts babble, icicles let go

their hold on peaked roofs,
pigeons scavenge
snowy wastes for oats.
The season runs the show

and now is the time
to fling open the doors of
stables and barns;
and no one's to blame

except the weather,
the rank breeze wafting down
from the heights:
the mounds of dung.

after Boris Pasternak

20

In the torrent

Downstream the raft plunged
in the pale gray of the foreign
shore, glittering,
receding, in the gray
of slanting surfaces, mirror
light flashing.
Borne down, the Baptist's
severed head, hair
matted, uprooted
where a hand's blue-tinged
loose nails scratched.

As I loved you, your heart
was unruly, the roast spitted on the beating
fire, the mouth, that poured open,
open, the torrent
came down and rose
with the herons, leaves
fell and filled its bed.

We bent down over the stunned
fish, wearing scales
trod the cricket's song,
over the sand, out of shoreline
arbors, we came
here to sleep, no one
walked around the bed, no one
put out the mirror, no one
will wake us
in time.

after Johannes Bobrowski

When the killing June sun is at its zenith, we head toward the pool hall's coolness which, unlike the swimming pools, to which we would repair, is not

OFF LIMITS TO CHILDREN

("But what if he promises not to jump in, splash around or go near
the diving board . . . what if he . . . proceeds in a
straight line back and forth propelled by fins and propped
above the blue by a darker blue kickboard . . . ?")

It's idiotic to argue with blind authority but I can't help myself. And this keeper of the gates says children "can swim in the pool as long as you stay with them and pay an $8 guest fee . . . an $8 guest fee." Put off by the repetition of the charge I still need those elements, air and water, to repeat my theme, since their material forms—cathedrals, pools, hotels, and seas—embody the contradictory necessities of life as I know it. In the unknowing brine of our remaining time.

21

Pool Hall

In the untenable
tenanted heat we hone our skills at pool
      since Amsterdam Billiards is the coolest
place I know this June in Manhattan

and brings me back
to Akron (where I have never been) (or:
      only passed through)
                        and my school-mates' stories
of just how tough and cool
          you had to be
to hang in Akron's pool halls,
      manhood's consummate test!—
consummatum est unless your nerves were match

for your skills; (the pool hall groupies,
girls—enterable if you won—
      beat somebody whose reputation etcetc . . .)

        but only
passing through Akron on my way west
    did I "get" why the McMann brothers,
hipster-greasers, chose to spend their youth
    indoors: because for dust and wind,
      absence, flatness, and slums,

for howling nothingness without the grandeur
    of desert or sea,
        Akron could not be beat.

I was surprised that my hand / eye . . .

    was active this

        five-in-the-afternoon,

taking fast aim, play-
ing quickly, though not so fast
as my—until this instant—right-handed son
who, playing lefty, knocks balls in from all
distances and angles . . .

       "Let's not keep score, let's just shoot,"
the little boy offers
in his—catastrophic—leap toward wisdom.

22

Before Summer Rain

All at once something
from the green world's gone;
something . . . the park comes right up
to the window—without a sound.

A plover whistles in the wood,
grave and urgent, like Jerome,
desert saint poised to translate
out of whiteness, skulls and bones,

whose effort the rain will echo.
The chateau walls, as if oppressed
by the brooding paintings in their frames,
recede; reluctant to hear our words betray us.

And the worn tapestries are strewn
with the off light of childhood
afternoons you feared would never end.

after Rainer Maria Rilke

23

Poolside

It's fun to use a pool illegally. To pull into a hotel parking lot, squeeze into your suit in the car, and waltz in with an easy, slope-shouldered gait. Then if a waiter appears asking if you would like anything at poolside to resist the temptation to begin a con, and in doing so, become one. (There are subtle differential ethical issues here.)

It's like kleptomania except there's no mania involved, only a desire for relief from the heat, or the boredom, horror, and monotony of existence . . . underscored by being on the road.

It's enough sometimes to pull off the road and dive in. Forget about swimming. I don't frequent hotel pools illegally for exercise, any more than a kleptomaniac goes in search of le mot blouse to match her new — skirt.

You think I'm impeaching myself, digging my own — grave —

when it's you who are on trial
YOU who set things up so that stratagems like this
come — to exist.

> You who set up dialectics as an
> argument someone wins and someone comes
> out looking — foolish —.

Further instructions:

The classier the place the easier
it is to con your way in by using
the distracted look of people to whom
a room key is a "Jesus I forgot . . ."
sort of object, and whose expression reads:

This life in the fast lane leaves me no time
to remember what state I'm in . . .

*—but now that I'm here can I get a suit
cleaned and pressed . . .*

"But sir, it's 10:45, I don't know . . ."

"There are . . . other hotels . . . next time I shall
consider the Plaza Athénée. . . ."

"It will be done. Before you can say—"

Elsewhere.

(O for the days when a hypersensitive
shortcircuiting system would be
sent like Thomas Mann
to spas that fostered . . . inactivity.

Strange, the biographies never mention
money. . . .

Nor do the novels. Lukács called Lawrence

and many other moderns

*onto the carpet for gliding over
these very details.*)

♣

(High Diversion: Cooling Off in the Pool at Stratton Inn After the
Women's Tennis Tournament)

When the sky to the north grew thick with cirrus,
each cloud identical yet distinct, like logs on a raft,
I remembered overhearing something about whirlwinds
and hailstones; roofs torn off; lines down.
Out of the question. Then
darkness dropped anchor and thunder
stunned the distance with such a ricochet,
it was as if, like a terrorist,

the tempest had taken control
of the resort's loudspeaker system.
I was torn between concern and the wish
for the storm to clear the air
of the future for the future.

❦

(Paying Guests: The Colonial Hotel, Brattleboro)

The outdoor hot tub is empty at nine
but for the three dusty travelers,
reconnoitering in water
under the vaporous charcoal of the night:

and yet those misty heights are restless,
the stars pulsing, swimming, kicking,
like an unborn child, to get out.

The jets churn the chemical water,
mimic the swirl of nebulae.

The jets consistent.
The swirls chaotic.

Nothing is far from anything.
Distance is a figment.

❦

In the Colonial Hotel in Brattleboro you can sit in the outdoor hot tub, a
rarity in New England, and gaze up at the stars. Only tonight there are
no stars. Just the hazy swirl of unlit cumulus.

As a boy I loved mud. The muddier I got the more I loved it. Then at
some point I became more fearful and fastidious, almost overly self-pro-
tective.

And today it came to me, as I deposited my glasses in a sneaker at the
pool's edge, that my fears grew in proportion to my lack of sight, natural

vision. Time and space blur, like a dusk of hummingbirds. My hesitation at the water's edge has everything to do with my growing inability to see without my glasses.

❧

"Precocity" (Sleepover Camp)

At the age of six
I was the youngest
little kid ever

to pass the swimmer's test,
which meant belly-flopping
from a viciously high

lifeguard's perch, suppressing
tears (can anything
hurt so much

and leave you without
marked internal damage?),
and continuing around

the roped off area.
There were no marks for form.
I say continuing so as not

to dignify my awkward
passage with a term
like swimming. Staying afloat

and moving through the water
at the same time is closer
to the truth—and fairly simple—

when you set your mind to it.
I wasn't courageous.
It didn't look high up

and the white wooden steps
were easy to ascend.
But when I looked down

I couldn't believe.
I didn't have the courage
to inch back down as the low

voices of counselors
and campers on the shore
carried across the water.

I had come to a decision:
The impact would hurt,
I would turn red and get

water up my nose; and rise
from the murky lakebottom
spouting, alive.

♣

There was no hot tub outside Woody Guthrie's shack in Topanga
Canyon. Only the tattered bark of eucalyptus trees. But the waterfall was
swell if you could go there alone, or with a woman, and not some acid-
headed goon. Not that I slept well, or slept at all. The cabin was bare
except for a few well-thumbed paperbacks.

Cat's Cradle Flew Over the Divided Self

They said that Woody holed up in the shack in Topanga to drink.

I found it hard to imagine him
binging within
the rough cedar
walls and floors,

and yet it seems right,
here in New
England, to listen to Ramblin'
Jack Elliot—(born

on a "ranch in Flatbush")
sing Lone Cat's
San Francisco Bay
Blues tonight.

Light pried upon your eyes in the curtainless cabin that had been awake
since dawn trapping heat while you slept in your own sweat, you heard a
slow moody strumming coming from the waterfall. Pulling jeans on over
nothing you jogged barefoot over the root-congested path and in no time
at all you saw a girl with short blond hair and freckles and an acoustic
guitar perched between the waterfall and the cave. You had met her in
Santa Monica the night before. How did she get here, even as a friend of
the friend who brought me here? She looked up as if to say, *you don't
have to stay, you don't have to go.* I found beauty in her expressionless sad-
ness. I listened to a few of her five-string-serenades and said I had to go.
"It's been nice knowing you," she said in such a childlike uninflected way
that I swallowed my urge to say I'd be willing to change my plane reser-
vation if she'd be willing to . . . hang with me—leave the canyon and get
back to the sea.

I knew enough to know there was something here I didn't understand.

§

After a year of misadventures, camping out with friends on St. Mark's
Place, Staten Island, and Brooklyn, trying out various Y's and the
Chelsea Hotel, I retrenched, and the next fall found a studio in the West
Village. Woody's daughter lived upstairs, in a duplex; a palace compared
to my garret. When I passed her on the stairs she was coming home,
plum tuckered out from eleven hours of dancing, and I was just going
out. She disappeared for weeks at a time and one dire February she lent
her apartment to a woman who worked for a record company (and for
the Guthrie Foundation—we would have a cure!). We listened to my
scratchy sleeveless Archive recording of Bach's concertos for harpsichord
and soon after that she "dropped in" with all the Bach cello concertos

Casals had recorded (six albums in a pristine white box with raised gold lettering)—ecstacy enough. Then, when I failed to pay the electric bill, for which I was sure I'd been grossly overcharged (could one month of winter heating equal a month's rent?), and Con Edison turned off the power, she said she was going to be on the road for a while, and handed me the keys to the pad. Without provisos.

These were among the nicest gifts I had ever received. (So what if they cost her nothing?) The cello suites form the best bridge I know between solitude and loneliness.

A good decade later, when I felt flush enough to splurge on my first "boxed set" (the Budapest string quartet playing Beethoven's late quartets), I thought of the woman, I saw her shuffling around the kitchen counter—and couldn't remember her name. But she was hardly ever there and left before winter was over.

⚜

Waterfall

At the meeting of the icy silences
At the meeting of the furtive glances
Abruptly
When a door opens on the starry deep
Abruptly
Traveled by rivers abandoned in metal
Under the crumpled trees which fall from your hands
Under the odor of mutilated plants which line the road
Everything in the air is tepid
Everything is chilled in the heart
The heat trapped in the wake of discord
Murder with gleaming teeth
When the blood has finished the winding of its loop

Not wanting to be glutted
Not wanting anything to die of hunger
Keep the fullness of life which cracks the barrier
We must risk a leap into the light
Smash the love which sifts coarseness from reality

Against the shrillness of the deafened word
From one fire of the rapids to another
When the echo rolls under the bridge and laments

I open my body to the sparkling sun
I open my eyes to the light of your mouth
And exchange my blood for yours in the groove of time
In sweeping strokes our life flows from stone to stone

after Pierre Reverdy

24

Gorge

And so it was I entered the problem of width and depth,
the knowable and the unknowable.
Propelled by an engine.
Who knew if the five-gear four-cylinder import,
salt-stricken, rust-consumed,
which had never known a passing gear
and whose glass hatchback shattered
at the mere provocation of letting it down,
had the reserves to make it up the hill?
A hill? Maybe. But there was nothing gradual
in what reared abruptly above eye-level to throw me back,
a hill whose violent vertical thrust
the mountains' mesmerizing green
might have kept me from seeing.

At bends in the road, verges,
I looked down and down at what went on and on.
If I had not lost my way would I have been
taken so unaware by this immense interior?
Below Route 103, which everyone must take
if they would reach Harry's Cafe
"right outside of Ludlow,"
the gorge grows. Torn
by the improbable scale,
I doubled back to ask directions
from the granitic gas station attendant in blues—
too caught up in the adding machine's
shoot-out-in-the-canyon ricochet
to look up when he growled:
go the way you were going, only further.

It's all right being lost in the heights, as long as
haze disperses when the sun scans the grass,
ignites the mirror-pan in the river,
turns the meadows crisp, the fields various,
as the interstices are filled

with miles of unbroken tree-line.
If I had turned back before
I might not have found myself facing
the shards of the Marquis de Sade's castle
or put my head through the jagged hole
in the sandstone wall to glimpse
the bottomless, inexhaustible blue.
It didn't matter if the way was up or down.
When I looked up, the sky had no bottom.

III

✤

MOTEL EN ROUTE TO

"LIFE OUT THERE"

The marsh was steaming in the strong sun, and the outline
of the Spy-glass trembled through the haze.
ROBERT LOUIS STEVENSON

. . . in my friendship with Gilberte, it was I alone who loved.
MARCEL PROUST

What mad pursuit.
JOHN KEATS

WOOD FLOORS

I

Unimpeachable skies.

Reluctant to enter the silence.

How did it feel to

Then or now?

put an end to these

Don't say it.

reveries.

Wood floors.

What's wood got to do with it?

No one asked you to come back.

There are—proper—occasions.

The futile search for intimate relations between disparate and
unrelated things.

You muttered something about the light
behind the stained glass windows
growing stronger as night comes on.

Appearing to.

I called no take-backs.

You interrupt before I've had the chance
to complete a thought.

A thought. Don't dignify it.
I talk eschatology and you
come back with wood floors.

It wasn't an answer to your question.
It was the floor's wood
which spoke through me then.
The shapes asleep in the grain.

You're good at getting out of corners.
You don't keep still.
But don't for one instant think
                    I
will be seduced
by the mystical angle you're procuring.

Always on sidestreets I see
bewildered dogs, limping, dragging mousetraps.

The tool is dangerous. But it liberates man from labor.

2

Lights inside appear to blaze more fiercely after dark.

Eyelids and petals close, and the thunder
of corrugated shutters is no more.

The light is not behind anything;
it is in the stained glass.

I leaned back against the front steps.

I was granted this luxury because the doorman
volunteered to play catch with my son
to spare my back.

98

One horizontal band of light
(a relief in this horizonless city)
glowed even in the luminous evening.

Most likely this light—is it for the dead?—
is visible at all times

from outside the confines

for anyone who cared to look,
to anyone who could be bothered

to lift their eyes unto these windows

beyond self-preoccupation, beyond duty

and the will

♣

My son had long ago moved right of my periphery
but I could tell from the doorman's
participation in this game of catch
that everything was all right with the world

the ball not yet freed from human hands
by the steepness of the street.

I watched so many people disappear
into their separate lives,

the lives they live as if they were
the first humans from earth
to wake to a hard cock and wet cunt
and wonder how it blossomed
independent of any design.

3

Take my wife.

You—take *her.*

She used to jog every morning—

ho—*hum*

without her clothes on in the kitchen.

She wasn't afraid of getting stuck by a sharp implement?

We lived below street-level. Windows for air.

Light?

From other sources.

Like the skylight.

The kitchen flowed like a tributary
into the living room. So while I stood

innocently by drinking the coffee
she, long before, had made, she—

gyrated in place.
Without staring, without even looking,

by virtue of good, well, better than good,
peripheral vision, it was given me to see her,

lithe lean long, limbs pistoning, eyes
wild, hair flying, shoulder to breast,

triangle stark within the whiteness of her skin,
glistening, radiant with sweat

in the light that poured in.

And because what she was doing had nothing to do with arousing you.

There may

be something to that.

Take it from me. I've been in this business a long time.

You must be rich by now.

Do you know what it   costs   to rent   this space?
I can barely   make the rent   even with all   the moneypouringin.

Speaking of—"pouring in"—
you could use better lighting.
I like your octagonal walls,
I only wish, when I came here,
at different times of the day or year,
the light might strike
different sides differently too . . .

Are you—light sensitive?

There may be something to what you said
because she didn't like what I was doing

what I wasn't doing

Which she communicated how?

Ferocity of look. The implicit *not now*
in response to the sexual vibes . . .

I wasn't aroused; I was overcome.

Are you sure her not wanting to have sex then and there didn't
serve as further enticement and make you want it all the more?
There was a woman who complained

to you?

*Indirectly. That you wanted it more when she had gone through
the necessary underrated labor of a woman dressing and was ready to
walk out the door.*

Now I know who you mean. I wanted her to stay away.

Why not tell her?

Knowing what I knew of her history
I didn't want to supplement her pain.

So this was a ruse, a way of covering up your contempt?

Let's get back to where we began.

🙙

It was, it would have been, a perfect fantasy scenario:
you have an appointment to meet a dancer at her loft

and you arrive a few minutes early and she opens
the door a crack and lets you in and says she is just

finishing . . . her barre exercises.
Sweat-radiant, the belt to her turquoise

terrycloth robe hangs limp at her sides and she keeps
her bare skin contained with folded arms.

You sense—smell—she'd been alone
and naked in the loft for a long time

and when she retreats to the studio
(even with the Velvet Underground on loud)

you hear the robe thud to the floor
behind the opaque glass door.

I couldn't see all that was on the other side
in relief, but when the dancer did some slow

turnouts it was like being let in to her
through her . . .

Her?

The word shivers me. In a way it was more
intimate than sex and got me hotter

than I wanted to be in the scorching heat.

She had other things on her mind than your tumescent dick.

LOVE'S WAY

Her name was Love. That was unfortunate.
And she had an unfortunate weakness
for the word in casual conversation.

Of which you would have liked to cure her.

Especially when she, who was so in touch
with her body she could feel her ovaries
move, was too in touch to let touch
proceed beyond the skin's surface; penetration
pained her to a depth she could not explain.

Love begged me to believe she loved me,
and wasn't amused when I joked that maybe
she and I could see each other for love
and spiritual communication
and I could see Janice for sex . . .

"Why do you have to seek release," she asked.
"It's better if you don't come."
(Pause.)
"Ancient Chinese wisdom."

Maybe it was the bitter karma of the woman
who had lent me the room
                              that would not consecrate jism.

Or that in Tantric lore the figurative and the literal are blurred.

♣

"What could be better than what we have now?"

Lying under these warm woolen blankets
while all around us   chaos   reigned   .

"Keep your jock strap on.

I'm getting my period."

(Between getting it and having it she disposed
of the next ten days and I'd known her less
than a week . . .)

Love blossoms quickly.

And the thought of making love to this
fair-haired, delicate featured, ethereal dancer . . .
incited me to grow
what I had always lacked:

patience.

Love wasn't my type
(too delicate)
and I loved her all the more for it.

Pursuit is destiny.

A mirage of desire.

(Would she think I was cheating on her if I masturbated
after she went to sleep?)

Love was hard to read.
Understand. Decipher.

But easy to love.

Her gaze like sunlight on a wall.

And came home
grocery bags overflowing with fresh
vegetables from Balducci's.

Your garret blossomed.

Love as metier.

Love as territory.

The vanquishing of February.

The black wet trees and nights like broken waterpipes.

There was nothing Love wouldn't do for love
but the buck stopped there.

Love had no reason.

Love opened her soul.

I believed in her love.

And you knew you didn't love Janice
no matter how wide and sweet her pussy
became, in the wild
ride of your nights

muttering "I wish the girls at the Evangeline
could see me now. . . "

This posed a quandary.

Was I in love with Love?
Or flattered and infatuated?

I had no way of knowing
where love would lead.

What relief to be with Janice
where all was clearcut
and reeked of sex.

How did you meet Love?

Waiting in line at Con Edison. They had turned off her power too.

And you first saw Madelaine among a group
of women on the beach

—the others, ravening after coolness,
deserted the scorched open spaces—

                    in the July
heat, and you were
                    lonelier than ever.

I thought you were going to say hornier.

I was . . . you were . . .

Crazed by Testosterone

Seeing her among the other women made her

all the more

desirable.

The faded jeans that were
too small for her
in all the right places—
flung across the beach chair.

Love shared her loft with another woman.

What went on between them?

Love never told.

When you tried to get her to be more graphic
she tapped her lips.

They weren't living together as a couple,
but sometimes they slept together
                                    when it was cold,
as young women often do . . .—

Did. Through the Victorian era. And under hardship.

But when I pressed for specifics, what they did at times . . . perhaps . . . to
comfort each other . . . love turned cold: "It's not for you to know."
Love's ways.

And it hurt the way love delivered that maxim
so coldly, in the midnight blue nights.

They were darker than that. And bleaker.

You'll never get wise to yourself. You were not obsessed with Love, the subject,
you were obsessed with changing the way you sensed she saw you, with mak-
ing her vision of you commensurate, if not identical, with your image of
yourself.

My inner self. Grant me that at least.

I do. Which makes it worse. For who sees
anyone as they really are? Aren't all
conceptions of self and other approximate?

The problem of other minds. A thorn in your side.

She wasn't your type.

Maybe . . . she was a tease . . .

108

And you like to be teased as long as there's

satisfaction. . . . In time.

That's patience.

That's ecstasy.

The very week you were

> divided

> *over Love,*

an early love called out of the blue
to say hello but she wasn't sure
she wanted to see you . . .

What could I say against our abortive romance—

to the weeping of guitar strings in the canteen— . . .

This was my best course and I hadn't even
signed up for it: she

rubbed your crotch

under the checkered table cloths

in the sequestered "mom and pop" Italian

place and when I could no longer

swallow

she smiled

(—a fanged smile—)

and took

her hand away

and looked you hard

   hard

in the eyes *a look which said*

get a grip—it's better this way—trust me—you'll get there

later

(the word I like least in the language)

 later

when we conned the desk clerk at the Arroyo Hotel
to hand over the key

(pining in exile from her car

delivered at her door the day of her sixteenth . . .)

before the posse of diverse authorities burst in.

Badges, night sticks, Walkie-Talkies.

The police were cool:
"There's nothing more to be done
than to issue a warning."

The school deputy barked
"You're both grounded . . . —"

A week later, Sheila, stiffening
against this outrageous punishment,
flew home to Detroit. . . .

Now she was at Teacher's College
and had her [life together]
and a [boy friend]
doing something with the law
so *seeing* me wasn't necessary . . .

Especially since she could sense your
avid desire to pick up
where you left off when still in
your teens,
                  and cut straight

to the luscious part
                  without . . . like . . .
wasting time . . . catching . . . up . . . .

I always believed we could catch up
later; that men and women could get to know
each other better afterwards.

If they were still talking.

Like eating naked together on the sofa

        with chopsticks

        after love

        after sex

It's then the unforced disclosure
        becomes possible.

Language of feet lightly rubbing calves.

Like her chatting away while she pees
with the door
open.

Candor of the body.
Ardor of the heart.

Internal

life . . .

Intimacy

in the casual, unself-conscious gesture.

Like pulling up her pantyhose.

—snap of elastic at the waist—

before leaving — for work.

When in the morning you are forced to go your
separate ways...

and you pull on your   yawn   male "attire"

to walk the streets in the August heat

no—until it was time for her to
—come home from work— . . . ;

or pulling off her tights after a run
sweating, and salty, and surprised
that you should look at her like that—

        with greed . . . ,

when you'd seen her so often with nothing on . . .

These transformations entice.

Even when there's nothing intended?

More so when there's no design.

No garter belt, no hose, no half-bra.

And while costumes leave me cold

    the small erotic twists in the shift,
the rustle of nylon when she—
    she—this
woman

crosses
      and uncrosses

her legs   —   makes me catch   —   my breath   —

LOVE'S MIRRORS

Crossing Astor Place that night
when love was elsewhere and the snow
slivered down in the spray

of streetlights, I saw a woman I had known before
and she said, yes, I remember you, and no
I don't want to go over to your house for coffee

now, but yes, I will meet you later,
(—that word again!—)
let me look at my appointment

book, next . . . Tuesday night say around
eight, at the Cedar? ("Later" sounded more
like a week to me.)

After the perfunctory catching up in the well-
enameled cedar booth, our dialogue
segued toward sex.

She was always more forward than me. (Or
Devorah Love. I loved loved loved that v . . . !)
"Do you have a ceiling mirror over your bed?"

I'd always felt retarded around this woman.
Long ago it was time to let go.
And yet it was she who first spoke to me, saying

we weren't like the others,
and she who fled down darkened corridors
when I, against my will, responded in an uncool

way, talking anxiously.
Now I lived in pride of my bachelor pad.
And now my spare studio above the Glori Bead Shop

furnished with second hand
office equipment—except for the bed—
was further diminished in size by her eyes.

She could have waited
until our first date was consummated
before insisting we multiply ourselves.

On a spiritual plane I wasn't averse
to multiplication through mirrors
(though her favorite author, not mine,

saged in his blindness that copulation and mirrors
were to be abhorred).
How could she be sure

our interfacing during intercourse
wouldn't quell and quiet her questing
spirit?

(Chantal)

While I was becoming re-acquainted with Monica, I was in the midst of a liaison with a governess from Toulon.

The governess from Toulon had weekends free. She put herself in my hands. Pleasant and polymorphous, she did anything I asked. This was thrilling until my fever for her began to subside.

My father, apprised of my interest in the Faust story, had provided us with tickets to Werther and Faust, both of which he had the wisdom to avoid.

SET DESIGN

What is it . . . ?
The *basso profundo* impersonating Mephistopheles
bearded, gray haired, past his 70th year,
rolled down the red carpet
garbed in his red robe —

If the wardrobe room
and set designers
wanted *hell* —
they have earned
eternal passage there
for the hubris of their
unearthly
perfection . . . —

The set designers of hell
happened — upon
        a miracle;

a set that was more
than a perfect sem-
blance; imitation—

but was the Husserlian thing—itself.

Hell a thing?

The place itself. Because that night,
(I think it was a cool Thursday in autumn,
the weather wavering in the inbetween,
because I, who am (—need I say it?—)
morbidly sensitive to barometric pressure,
had nothing on over the subdued red-gold-purple
sports jacket I had bought (cut-rate)
after hours at the rack at Orbach's . . .
and Chantal had nothing on over her

deep turquoise cash-
mere turtleneck . . . ?)

Or an early spring night? Around Maundy Thursday . . .

while smoke billowed up from trap doors

and every time   the singer stepped onto the stage
Kleig lights heated up the infra-
red carpet,

and the antique baritone, tall, gaunt, hollow-cheeked

with the fakest beard ever glued to chin
of man,
       thudded to the red carpet and: flopped
from step to step,
       limp as a slinky,
as if the edge of each stair was moving towards him . . . —

the musicians sawing away in the orchestra pit,
to pump up the action—

and each descent to the next plateau
brought bravos from the crowd,

who now rose,
drowning the drum's thunder
with thunderous applause.

But was it for the fall or was it because
the singer's brittle bones
militated against such recklessness, such risks;
or for the execution of
the *fall* itself, or—the whole performance?

Like all bored people, I cast a critical eye
on the debonair audience:
custom-tailored suits, cruel glitter of jewelry.

I hated Gounod and wanted to go,
but could not pass through
              the rows of standing ovationers,

some of whom had snored—until this moment.

Dandruff poured like snow from the hair
of the exhausted husband in front of me.
I had watched his progress, or regress, towards sleep
whenever I grew bored with the spectacle.
His head lolled against the seat-back,
until, given a sharp jab in the ribs he sat
bolt upright, dredging, as if from the bicameral mind,
the posture his body had often rehearsed
in the military, in the Ivy League.

But the singer did not rise. He had died.

—*And you attribute this to set design?*

And the too-red redness. And the trapdoor
fumes. And his robe: it should have been
              cool red.

                              ⚜

I wonder if they knew just how fussy
Goethe could be about questions of harmonics.

Or plants: that a leaf may be
converted into any organ.

And any organ into a leaf.

Metamorphosis over taxonomy.

I don't know, but it was only after this night at the opera
that she wanted mirrors on the walls,
          and bathroom ceilings,
                        and lights installed

so we could watch ourselves
            watching ourselves
      make love;
                  —Had I ever?

Life is a series of crises in which X
forces its way to the center and hounds Y.

Now I've lost track of which woman.

Reconstruct?

I had gotten back in touch with Monica
during the time I was "seeing" Chantal.

That's no answer

But it's all you need to know.

—For now.

SOHO: THE EARLY DAYS

"—men, men, men,
who will come after them?"
OSIP MANDELSTAM

I miss living downtown. I could have bought a loft in 1977 for $27,000.
A thousand a year for every year of my life. Unattainable sum. And the
neighborhood was bare and barren except for fashion.

Tree houses built atop platforms.

The raft of future trust funds.

Promise of gulls over green water
in spring.

I remember the week when the loft was offered because Phil Ochs had
only just hanged himself and at the party a redhead named "Jo" beat her
fist against the misty windows, thick and round as portholes, keening her
lament over his death.

It seemed as if every other woman in the room had just broken up with
the guy who was giving the party. He was a grip; no, a gaffer; no, a sound
man—and he kept yelling that anyone who rode the subway on a daily
basis without earplugs was a fool. The loft was soundproof. Had I
noticed? I kept losing myself amidst the foliage in this indoor savannah,
this jugular jungle, the macaws and parrots raucous in the rubber trees.

It was hot enough to grow orchids. "$27,000 seems like a lot, but it's
nothing. I mean . . . you'll . . . (searching now for the right multiplicand)
. . . quadruple your investment in no time." "That's a lot to figure in your
head," I wish I'd had the wit to say. Instead I muttered something that
led him to add: "You don't need it all up front."

I don't mean to put him down. The woman who'd brought us to this
place—who was rounding up the cash to finish a documentary on

women in prisons (and another "ex" of our host's)—briefed us in the elevator that he'd "done sound-work for . . . de Palma and Scorcese."

🌣

In those days I often
            went places
                        with my lover
and an unattached
            female friend
                        who went in the hope of "meeting someone";

and—let's face it—having a good time and being in our good
                        company was just pretext, convenience;

more or less.

It was the dawn of a new age
in which there were more
available women than there were
men alone . . .

Where are the men?

A chant would go up.

The role of chaperone is one
I determinedly shed.

Though I did draw pleasure from the well
of listening to my lover and the other

woman evaluate all the relevant
males later when we three

repaired to more intimate
surroundings (northwest of Washington

Square) to release the eerie strangeness
of having been too long among so many

strangers, of having imbibed
not enough liquor and too much

of their anger sadness thwarted
ambition and panic as they

steadied themselves against the age
they were about to become

closing in like the narrowing
walls of this loft in the winter fog.

♣

Why the redhead?

My mother's mother had red hair.

The impossible copper of Courbet's "Jo."

("Like everything Venetian one had dreamed of,"
wrote Whistler, who'd had her before.)

Tousled, long and loose, she combed it without end
before the mirror.

She never cut it.

I try not to think about what my mother's life might have been like had
her mother lived.

The grandmother you never knew.

A Jew and a Christian scientist
she managed to inhabit the worst

of both worlds; told her daughter
not to call a doctor until the poison

from her leaking appendix
had done its work.

Watching her turn green as a Venetian lagoon
would not have been fun.

Maybe that's why the loft party scared you.

EASTER WEEKEND IN DENVER

I

Night in the high chaparral.

Intimations of ecstasy.

Before us in the misty.

Were it not for the wreck.

The white compact rolling into the ditch.

The wheels spinning in emptiness.
The radio screaming between stations.

The two young women, reeking of liquor,
hanging upside down
in the rat-colored light.

Torn stockings.
White dresses.
The heavy scent of hairspray.

They looked an awful lot like each other.
Remnants of blondness.

American beauty.

Running aground.

I can't remember—were they sisters?
Or inseparable friends?

2

A story about an accident.

A series of accidents.

How deep was the ditch?

Deep enough to conceal a car,
standing on end; and when I descended,

clambered down with desperate haste
to intervene . . . I could touch,
but not look over, the topmost ridge—

Your guide behaved too much like a gentleman now.

(The Bonanza Airlines turboprop
on which I would depart at noon
already on its way to the airport . . .)

I wanted more time alone with Dominique.

But you knew it was history.

But I didn't want to leave. I wanted to stay. And be

in Dominique's company.

Barry felt you, you and she, shouldn't be denied
this chance for a Brief Overcoming of Surface Differences

        (White Collar Jewish Boy
meets
        Blue Collar Catholic Girl)

More a tale of connection than sexual outcome.

Prelude to the end of friendship
that blossomed between two Jewish boys
away at school in the Sonoran desert.

3

(Maundy Thursday)

We parked only in high rock-studded spaces.
Disastrously jagged, beautiful; not true.

In search of isolated places in the heights he tore,
with radial tires indestructible, through rank thickets.

Heights provide the essence of illusion.
The far off looks both smaller and closer than it is.

Cliffs jutting over—nothing—; sleek abysses,
predatory by virtue of their inhuman patience.

4

Only when the car stopped did we release our embrace, and talk; the
    four of us.

Our talk ran into the night, quietly,
picked up by the echoing streams in the canyons.
On these cloudy nights the moon was watchful but shy,
clearly present behind the cloud-mat;
it raced along with us wherever we went.

The moon, swollen
on the horizon's rim.

Who looked at the moon?

Everything faded but the landscape of her body.

5

(Good Friday)

The sun never came out once all weekend.

No seizures in the forest to the scherzos of bluejays.

No ecstasy on the pine-needle floor of a cathedral woods.

And you trusting to your mischievous guide.

Between the doeskin covered bucket seats
I saw the hair at the nape of Inger's
neck, the thick blond tresses caressing
her ears. Sex was so hard to get
at 16, and Barry was already in the groove,
just as suave (to borrow the name of a popular
clap-colored hair lotion of the time) as he boasted.

Getting sucked off by a wig, or a real girl?

Without having to move a
muscle, to do anything reciprocal

—except to keep his foot on the gas
and his hands on the wheel.
His eyes were and were not on the road.
His eyes were everywhere.

Coming, he angled the rear view mirror
so I could see his eyes roll upward before he winked.

—A violation.

(Dominique missed this display,
her head buried in my shoulder.)

6

His Denver stories were so compelling.

*He made promises, what's more
he kept them, fixed you up
with the woman of your dreams,
an olive-skinned Italian Catholic knockout
with libertine
tendencies whose boyfriend was conveniently out of town
between Maundy Thursday and Easter Sunday . . .*

Deep down I never dreamt she

would be interested in me.

He transformed you into an object of desire for her.

Something like that.

You couldn't believe she would take to you.

*And look at all the J.A.P.s—I mean,
nice Jewish girls.*

*From whom you ran.
To escape suffocation.*

Expectation.

*Which made the perversity of his setting you up
all the more scandalous; magnificent;*

*(redeeming him from the banality he had no desire
—as he posited his future—
to overcome, much less elide, sidestep, or . . . transcend . . .).*

7

Your friend is the magus of the operation.

He poured such mythical material into our ears
we were primed for action, and since his girl
friend, fiancee rather, and this girl
were best friends, inseparable,

> and *she tells him everything*

(and hearing it from Inger is as good as hearing it from her . . .)

there's a high degree of truth, or at least fact,
in what he knows and

shamelessly

tells: that while Dominique is utterly faithful
to the all-around guy whose ring she slides off

and loses, somewhere in the rumpled nest of the back seat

and while he's the only boy with whom she's gone "all the way,"

Barry feels that because they too
are likely to get hitched while still in their teens
that she owes herself this experience:

everyone should sin.

(Or he owes her. Or he has her vicariously through you. Or: . . .)

My desire wasn't centered—my whole body
thrilled—tingled just to "hold her hand"—

And while you did everything but "it"

I was still stunned, overcome when I unbuttoned her jeans
and felt her wet heat that went on forever as she appeared
to come and come again against my exploring hand. . . .

She and I were wrapped in an embrace when the dark miracle took
    place.

My shock when I rose from the swelter of her lips to catch
my breath—to catch—our reflection in the rear-
view mirror; which he had angled
down, to catch our every action.

8

The two incidents
occurred almost simultaneously.

I couldn't believe how ill my luck could turn.

We had spent days

        your lives

building up to it.

Your problem is that you always forget
what led up to it,
or the times before (and after) that you were borne away
by a giddy, delirious freedom with a girl
you had met away from school or home,

on one of your winter escapes to Florida
or the tropics with your father

between the palms, banyans and bananas,

secure—though you didn't know it—
in the built-in brevity of the encounter.

Ten Days on a Surfboard on the Pacific
returning to your room only to crash and eat

and see how Dad was making out.
(Dad: the most sorrowful word in the language.)

This was just a more intense version . . . —

All those midnight beaches.

The murmuring foam of wave and cloud.

The dust of yellow cabanas smelling of Coppertone
which the Jews rubbed on like freedom.

9

You drew a lot from this one Long Weekend in Another Town.
She saw you as you felt you deserved
to be seen; or as a creature worthy
of a lovely young woman's desire and cheer.

I was no longer who I was before we set out
into the awkward weather, the comfortless
monochromatic haze; the low
visibility turned my gaze toward
Dominique again; annihilated
small talk: we were confined together

with a mix of wonder, desire, and raw
need—to go further with another
human being than would have seemed possible
a mere 36 hours before . . .

And your last hours with her

squandered

helping these two victims of the crash

whose breath smelled of liquor

undergo a going over at the hospital.

Our time ended just before.

The obscenity of the rearview mirror turned down.

Payment extracted for fixing us up.

It's a sort of prince and the pauper story. In case you're about to ask who was who I can tell you that my cousin was a JAP of the highest order.

By that do you mean his mother made sure before he left the house that he "had enough money" and stuffed $20s into the pockets of his Brooks Brothers corduroy leather-armpit

elbow

jackets; he didn't have everything; he had duplicates, triplicates, back-ups for every emergency; preparing for his junior year

(of high school)

abroad he carried a separate suitcase with razor-blades, soap, and toilet paper...: not for him to wipe his ass with the sandpaper that is the standard in European toilets or the torn out pages of a paperback he had finished...(as did Luis Bunuel's grip during the filming of La Cuisine Bourgoisie *with Ross MacDonald's* The Chill*).*

Of what writer did he not have the complete works in complete sets, many first editions . . . ?

And so it comes as no surprise to you—as it did to me—that in one vertical stack in his closet he had every issue of Playboy *that had ever appeared in order "of appearance . . ."*

which I quickly leveled . . .

What were you doing there rummaging through your cousin's possessions?

My father had custody of me in the summers.

Only I wasn't allowed to stay with him.

The court decreed you were to stay with his sister.

And her husband Jack.

Which was Jake with me since they had the most powerful
air-conditioner in Gotham City,
and a live-in-French-Canadian maid, named Lucille—
    who brought the pauper breakfast on a tray—

cereal, eggs, toast, bacon, chocolate milk
        a feast for the gods!

And for two or three—give or take—weeks a year,
I had no one to answer to until my father
got off work or my aunt
requested my presence at

        LUNCH — . . .

                            ❧

All day I lay in bed and read
        Playboy. Shaw's stories weren't half-bad.
Earnest. Moral Seriousness with a touch
        of eros. Just a touch!

                            ❧

*". . . and her hips swung boldly because she was a dancer and also because she
knew Michael was looking at her."*

"The girls in their . . ."

How dare—

It just slipped out.

Girls? Girls? Girls?

You mean: young women.

Girls of Slender Means.

Body.

"Being."

Women walking alone or with anticipation's quick stride
fluttering the light flowing cotton of their skirts,
the labial petals and eyelids on their skirts,

the wind moving in and under.

I watch the small breeze ruffle
the lake of—cloth where it
collapses between the thighs—

when it might have been leg-motion
that caused this ripple to pass
along the dappled surface. . . .

There is something beautiful about the way

   women walk in summer
in their longing to be free
   of heat, let in
as much as can
   pass through the tunnels
of sleeveless blouses and careless bras . . .

Why couldn't you have said it that way
   in the first place?

There is no "first place," and
   without remembering I was remembering,
I was remembering the title of a story
   by Irwin Shaw.

"The Girls in Their Summer Dresses"

A macho ski-bum and sports enthusiast who tossed away a career
writing serious literature for blockbusters that could be
converted into mini-series.

Maybe. But I love to say it:
"The Girls In Their Summer Dresses."

But you read him in your cousin's Playboy*s.*

And every time my faking an ailment worked
to keep me home from school, the one movie
on TV I hoped would brighten the day had to be
an unreal version of Shaw's "Tip on a Dead Jockey"—
gamblers' binoculars aimed at dubbed hoofbeats.

※

There's a way men have of looking at women
that's not quite so feral, so predatory

as you think, a glance held
no longer than a footstep, her body

taken in whole; taken
in.

Fluttering in the loose dresses of the breeze.

※

You'd say I "masturbated."

I'd say I learned how to delay orgasm,
apply Tantric practices before I'd heard the word,
learned not to blow my wad over the babe
of the month . . . and to find
ways through the centerfold . . .
to the rare, quieter portraits . . .

I took my time
before inaugurating the ceiling with my jism.

Impressive. You can only do the former once.

What would you do after you came?

Come again.

But in the time between?

Read the stories.

♣

"You look at every woman that passes."
"That's an exaggeration."
"Every woman."

"The Girls in Their Summer Dresses," Irwin Shaw

♣

I became harder to satisfy.

There was much I could not reconcile.

The comfort *Playboy* offered
was cold indeed,
                    when it was my luck,
on a blind date—to meet a girl
                    who entered
my heart by a gesture she made
        in the rain . . .

a girl so tall, dark, severe
        and intelligent—yet light-hearted too—!

. . . *served as your Introduction to Heartbreak.*

I wouldn't put it that way.

Nor would "I," but there you have it.

I forgot. In the humid air of early summer

I went to work at my father's office,

and in the back room met a bright, preppy hep-cat,

   who could see I was, like, a little bit   lost,
or—at LOOSE ends . . . ;

   alone in New York knowing no one my age—
except the disappearing children in suburbs
   with mystical place-names
like Great Neck, Harrison, Teaneck, and New Rochelle

I had known over the seven summers I'd spent at sleepaway camp
for which I'd flown east from the time I was five.

For it was not the children who had disappeared, but their childhoods:
they had become consumers, avid wearers of mohair cardigans, anticipa-
tors of cars their upwardly mobile parents would hand over to them the
moment they reached driving age in the east.

He—his name was Peter—said, "I have someone you would like."

And when I came in Monday he said, "So what did you think of—"
It was on my face. I didn't have to say a word.

"I knew it . . . ," and while she

consented to go out with me
several times afterwards,
   she, like every girl who ripped
my heart out of my chest— cavity —

had a boyfriend lurking,
revving up the engine of his Thunderbird.

It felt good to make her laugh.

Walking west on 57th St. after two lovely hours
sharing armrests in a theater's dark
and a drink at the Regency Bar

I looked up at the sky.
Clouds passed like riderless horses.
I think it's supposed to rain, I said;
    or—it's raining—and held out my palm
to test the   precipitation factor—:
    she held her palm out too;
    we laughed, and I took
her hand—and it was—*great*!

She was the ruin of your solitary reveries.

No longer content with image; you wanted flesh.

And that was trouble city in that time and place . . .

The weather was uncertain. Another person might have taken an umbrella . . .

She had terrific posture, yet did not hold herself
like a rod, like my English teacher sophomore year in Salt Lake
who, when she announced her marriage to a suitor we had not
laid eyes on, maddened the males in the class.

Who started butting the walls making mean remarks about her posture and
what they'd like to do to her. Most disapproved of sex before marriage but the
thought of this marmoreal, righteous, precise, upstanding, chestnut-haired,
freckled, pretty young woman being fucked was a little hard for the guys to
take in. Not after all the joking about her being a virgin and everything. The
idea of a sexual life burgeoning within this "cool exterior" was hard to take.
What were the larger implications? So cool and yet—so hot? Hot enough to
want to get married, to want to get fucked.

To fuck.

I didn't know how much I disliked the answer "no"
until Laura made it clear I was out

of the picture.

But she did it more masterfully than that
ordering her mom to say she wasn't home or

at an hour when she HAD TO BE HOME
refusing to come to the phone—

and when, to get me off her case she lifted
the receiver to her shapely, her

incomparable ear, and condescended to say yes to my
"Laura, is that you?"

she let the silence resound

she held the note of silence

she let me blunder and err and utter the futile question

in a voice by now fraught with tension

but unwilling to give in

"When can I see you again?"

to get an answer that went   something like

"I don't want you to call—."

"But I thought we had such a good time."

"I can't talk. I'm off to Princeton
for the weekend. I think I see his Porsche—..."

As if she were leaning out the window of her high rise
phone in one hand, binoculars in the other,
like the suspect gamblers at the track.

*Literature did not come to your aid. You had no "Billy Budd" to help
explain your stutter*

the rush of flooded consciousness

utter voicelessness

Stuttering would have seemed like eloquence
compared to this zeroness

alone—my hand holding the phone—in my cousin's palace—

every pore-cell   screaming

a heaviness beyond   —

time to   —   die

Because I was sure there was a misunderstanding at the core: her choice
of him over me had purely to do with externals: age, status, possessions.
How could she *let me die* just to have the warm wind in her hair on the
freeway: just to be

in the company   —   of this tweedy, penny-loafered *jerk*.

"Maybe *during* the week."

"He's giving me his ring this weekend."

He's a dead man. He's dead. He'll never draw another breath. You think
they let Bugsy Siegel live just because he drove cool cars and knew the
need of the American people for a neon wilderness?

♣

So what if she was more mature—most girls are—
but why couldn't she let me catch up, why

couldn't we plan to see each other when I
was in the East and see how it went, why

when I knew she'd never duplicate
the bliss of standing in a waterfall in mid-Manhattan

laughing in the rain
that wasn't even falling?

Even if you're correct in your diagnosis that the good feeling
between you was in itself mutual you're wrong about all else.

⚘

But did you value the girls who fell for you?

Value!

Did you return their . . . affection?

It was my misfortune to like so and so more more than I loved her . . .

——

Don't interrupt! They would have given me up anyway once they found
out what I was really like at the time.

We'll come back to that.

Let's stay with our suspicion that any woman
who made her interest in you clear to you
was automatically suspect, as if
there had to be something wrong with her
if she   really   liked   you—

And for the very qualities that Laura overlooked.

Couldn't see.

Overruled en route to her decision to ink you out.

All of her.

And you're sure her cold
shouldering you was not foresight
of the insecure life she'd be forced to endure
with one who would not become
a doctor or lawyer or "executive"?

Are you sure her prescient turning away
was not a form—of protectiveness?
Are you sure it was you—(at-the-time) she scorned
or a future it was not-in-her-to-will,
a future shorn of the good things
    she'd grown up on.

"Grown accustomed to."

Drinks at the Regency bar.

I took her there—

The intervals between each plunk of the piano keys.
"Where one relaxes
on the axis
of the wheel of life . . ."

But that was a one-shot deal: an underage boy proving he could
get served at a fancy bar.

And she, she was underage too.

But no one would have dared to card her.

No, no one.

♣

After all this I don't feel like I've quite gotten her:
Goethe says, "One cannot speak without beginning to err."

AESACUS, THE DIVER

His birth was a mystery.
Spoiled by the shady groves

in the mountain heights,
young Aesacus ranged the hills.

His conditions of happiness
were simple, in theory:

life in the open air; contempt
of ambition; the love of one woman

to people his solitude.
Often on his rounds he saw

Hesperie, the river god's
daughter, but when

he caught her alone, off-guard,
drying her hair in the sun

still wet, still clinging
to reverie, he gaped:

his gaze intent, his lust feral—
(as once, upon arriving in London

in the drought of mid-July, I had no sooner
set my bags down on the luggage rack,

than I saw a woman across the running
pinks and grays of the roofs and walls—

handsome, short-cropped chestnut hair—
walk to her window

and with a sleepwalker's unswerving, even tread,
hook her thumbs under the hemline of her nightgown

and pull it over her head).
She sensed his presence

and when she zoomed in on his face
in the stark light-dark of the leaves

she panicked—crashed through thickets
to the barely traveled road

where a driver hit his brakes—too late.
Aesacus held her mangled body in his arms

and keened his lament; how could one
outburst of irrevocable lust—

which shocked him as much as her—
poison their lives forever?

(Her reaction puzzled me—
I hadn't volunteered

to wash the remaining sand off her body
to make sure no glass had wedged its way

into the calluses on her feet
on her earlier crossings of the jetty—

she'd volunteered to give me a "tour"
of the musty shower room where the four

dancers hung their leotards
before they stepped into the stall;

but when I put my arms around her waist,
loosely, the way her mosaic-patterned sash was tied,

she held her body taut, her cheekbones tight.
I was so taken with the angles of her face

with her hair pulled back like that
I didn't care if she wanted to kiss me or kill me.

And though my gaze made her uneasy
she would have been angry if I had never called.)

He ran toward the high cliff,
worn thin at the base by rasping waves,

and made a running jump, as if
to free her with his own ruin.

No one cuts a more ludicrous figure
than a failed suicide.

But it wasn't his fault:
the reclusive Tethys

caught sight of the passionate
youth flailing the air and—

in a fit of misplaced compassion
for the wild boy's bad luck—

stuck a life-jacket on his back,
so as he strove to reach the bottom

and stay below, his heartbeat easing
to the rate of dolphins and whales, each stroke

bringing him closer to the giddiness
before asphyxiation, he felt himself drawn

upwards, spewed
into the ambiguous charity of light.

Again and again,
he dashed his body into the sea

but each time, however deeply
he thrust himself downwards,

he was restrained, held back
by the vest attached to his scapula—

like the wings of his own
desire . . .

It's hard to die when something
stronger than death holds you to life.

Many who found their way to that sparse rockface
mistook the diver for a cormorant;

and in time, he came to be known as—
The One Who Struggled to Stay Below the Waves.

after Ovid

AESACUS RISEN

It is always strange to guess
how people know what they know,

but it was no
accident that Paris was the only

one of Aesacus' brothers
who didn't show up at his funeral.

Did he know the tomb was empty?
And that the mourners had been misinformed

and should have looked—seaward . . . ?
Can Paris' absence at Aesacus' grave

be explained by his hatred of the youth
who foresaw Troy's ruin in

the beck of his lust and advised
that he should die

when he hit the air?
It's doubtful his parents,

well-intentioned, shrewd,
informed of the dangers

of poisoning children's minds,
let him know of this interchange;

yet Paris knew something—knew who
stood between him and his calling—

knew with whom, among his many brothers,
he had to contend. The war

might have gone the other way
had Aesacus lived—stayed in human form

to don armor; or he might have made things worse;
confounded Trojan morale with disdain

of group decisions.
Aesacus would not have seen a reason for living

in a demoralized world, just because Ovid claimed
he "*could* have fought like Hector."

AESACUS AND THE DANCER

Why? Why think incessantly about women?
Lips, eyes, hair; hair everywhere,
and the shadowy opening as she lies,
leg raised, heel planted on the sheet.
What went through her mind on the dance floor
during a split? Did her labia open, like an eye?
Or did she have a kind of detachment
from the pleasure of her body
so that for him to stiffen while she was rehearsing,
or padding absently around the loft
with the tampon's tail dangling
from the furze of her triangle,
were somehow at odds with the sweet
tacitness between them during sex,
how she angled her pelvis to take him in.

MIXED MESSAGES

When you shacked up with Samantha on Schermerhorn
she walked around in the buff
and it turned you off.

Sexual harassment.
We were mere roommates.

And prior to that, classmates.

She knew you'd spent the worst part of a year
looking for a place to live
and when you turned up for class
pale and hoarse
muttering about the waste of life
she said she lived in a house with four
other women in Brooklyn and if it was
all right with them for a man to you know
break the semi-random symmetry
she would share with you her top floor
apartment though you should understand
it was really too small for two people
who weren't really intimate
but she'd be willing to do it if
she could do what she always did
like walk around naked

"If it's not a problem for you."
I started to say "How could it be" and said "Of course *not*."

And of course this thought that she and I might have it off *did* flicker for
an instant in my brain and of course I switched it off . . . — *not* because I
feared she might get the wrong (or right) vibe, but because

something about Samantha made me wary.

Like a fool at a smorgasbord, I ignored my unease
and agreed to the usual "split household expenses down the middle."

Samantha came and went in this or that stage of undress and I didn't
    look twice —
proud of my reserve,

(a welcome respite from a life spent in ardent pursuit);

and spring had come to Brooklyn; Hoyt Street paraded its magnolias;
the year's

tensions began to unravel as I drowsed, book in hand,
on Samantha's couch, while the smell of flowers

wafted up from the garden below and the sunlight poured
in through the window,

and each particle of dust danced, lit up like fireflies—

sparks striving to maintain altitude.

Spirits inhabit the flames; each
swathes himself with that which burns him.

❦

Until Samantha opened the blinds that morning I hadn't known what
grandeur lay beyond

the fire escape's transparent weariness and dust,

what magnificence the anxious season kept under wraps
until now, and how wonderful it was that she had placed the couch in an
    incongruous

nook—a pure unnamable space—

(that would have confounded the most unscrupulous
landlord's attempt to call it a half-room, or alcove . . .),

blessed with the grace to let light shower in, pour, flood

the area, without blinding us, without the hot house

effect that leaves you in a sweat and sends

you reeling toward the shadows or the deep

recesses of the cave . . . —

Why bring that in?

Sweating it out?

She and I were both wrestling with Plato
in the heat of the seminar room, glistening with sweat,
sitting tight as we tried to think—to reconcile:

the ancient Greeks, the riots in the sheets,

> *streets*

dialectics, wave particles, the phenomenology of mind

as contradiction, as

embedded in Rameau's infantile antics

in mimicry becoming other ingesting selfless

mirror stage everything permitted scarcity "no longer a problem," praxis
     slow

to evolve.

I could not want someone so avid in wanting to be wanted —

Immeasurably less pain if money had been the source of our tensions!

Samantha flaunted herself.
You averted your eyes, rather gazed
upward, toward the floor above,
  where Martha the librarian
      lived alone
  with the Collected
      Everyone
  in paperback
and, confess, your yearning for her brought back
  earlier torments.

You roused in her a kind of fear.

You didn't have to lay a hand on her
for her to register the other
    message: sheer
want; unsheathed desire.

In pure form, the distillate—

And you were too young—

Age has nothing to do with it—

To know—

You never know—

That terror is part

Inexorable—

Inseparable—

Of what you feel

In beauty's grip

"I lived at the end of beauty's reign . . ."

※

Sex with the librarian would have been
like a conversation in tongues, the best

kind!

※

We talked about books.

No, you talked. To cover up your nervousness. A tactic that . . .

don't remind me . . . I'm still embarrassed. . . .

*You didn't behave badly. You behaved terribly. Samantha was thrilled to
discover that you were revolted by her and waited, panting, for the librari-
an's footsteps on the stairs.*

※

Women are divided.

In body.

Men.

In mind.

The simplism of that

   terrifies me

the silence

   of bound horizons

makes me feel

hemmed in

the world is a prison

when I am far

from what I love . . .

🌹

I'd find myself innocently flipping through . . .

There's nothing innocent about anything you do . . .

But I wasn't looking for . . .

Aware of . . .

A lingerie catalogue came in the mail—

addressed to you no doubt—

No. To my—

Then why did you feel compelled to look through it?

I like to.

*But if you found yourself in that section of a department store
you   lingered . . .*

to maintain that tingling, the roots-of-your-hair sensation.

The dry air empty again without her.

*And if someone you knew were to call your name
     you'd jump— . . . guilty, unfocused, distracted—
as if caught committing a crime.*

No, but it was the single intense
    focus of this catalogue:
that women feel this pressure

to attract men. And keep them.
    A force every inch as
predatory as the male gaze.

The catalogue has women in poses
    more erotic than in
magazines meant for men's consumption,

where the model parts her vulva
    as if asking you to look
through it as through a keyhole

which it does not resemble
    unless the top
of the keyhole is parallel

to the hood of the clitoris.

                    ♣

Road-weary, I paused at a truck stop.
The women's magazines
on the crowded rack all had

lingerie features—.

Generational?

The girls I knew in high school
and college and grad school
wore so little underneath
their skirts and shirts, little time
was spent on the time between
becoming intimate
and becoming—more—intimate . . .

And after years of that
the integer of children
made time stand between ourselves
and these "mature" ecstasies.

No—lingerie—no—lingering

No—whiling hours away—

Pining

Love-

sick

And the mannequins talked back.

♣

Prompter

Then the volume of erotica arrived.
Was it a sign? The woman

doing so many things to the other
woman, finding her way into one

hole with her tongue, another
hole with her finger when her lover

called out ah, ah, (deep
sigh of release, momentary suspension

of pain and plunder, war and hope,
of kitchen chores accruing, of am-

bivalance dissolving, the knot
itself dissolving), the woman

on the chair, the standard issue
Samsonite they drag out

when the congregants exceed the pews
over Easter and Passover,

begging now for her
not to stop, (skirt yanked to hip,

no time to strip) and I understand
even though I'm a man, I feel the same

longing warming me in being
about — to come — the same

suffusion of self-forgetfulness
which love is.

It was one of those parties where the older people who had all done inter-esting things talked together awkwardly, muttering ephemeral phrases, and I found myself—balancing my buffet supper on my lap—across from the boyfriend of the granddaughter of the guest of honor. (She was elsewhere being ogled.) He had just taken a course on cross-dressing and while real-life experiments were not required she thought he should try it anyway. At this point she rose from where she sat on the white sofa between two dignified presences in dark blue suits and joined us. "I rum-maged through my closet and laid my clothes down on the bed for him to try on." And he said: "It was something to put on her dress. I could never have guessed how exposed and vulnerable I'd feel."

The whole notion of opening your legs endlessly,
and letting another body into your body
is so wonderfully intimate—:

why are there so many women alone?
who can bear to leave them alone?

Women are mortal: every minute their bodies
are reminding them of something to be done.

⚘

"No," the student continued (having read your thoughts?), "my *chest.* I
didn't need breasts . . ."

To feel how women feel.

Like a gorge which surprises itself with its own immensity.

Pushing through the questions of dimension.

⚘

Stealing a glance at her looking at herself in the mirror.

"Can't I ever walk around naked in my own home
without you—or take a shower without you—
or slip out of my pantyhose without—"

> your love

The mounded tuft packed down and in
behind the diaphanous nylon gear
women wear.

Tee shirts, jeans, straplessness,
ankle-length or mid-thigh skirts.

One is no less erotic than the next.

⚘

Dryness and tingling,

Wandering Sunset—alone—

Let down and down

By the barren hollow facades—

The celeb emptiness—

The characterless structures

Thrown up overnight

Asked to stay forever!

Ciro's and the Brown Derby

Like diarrhea

In the light

Of day, the lusterless

Gravel, and acned attendants

Suiting up in white

On white

For the night,

Impassive, anonymous,

Like the wrong woman.

♣

*And Samantha was so put off you didn't
want to watch her take a bath she said,*

"This isn't working out. I want to you to leave."

And so it was back to the Chelsea Hotel.

Everyone on acid.

Pinwheel eyes.

MOTEL EN ROUTE TO "LIFE OUT THERE"

for the left-handed woman

I

"Women are getting better and better"
"or worse and worse"
"at pointing out"
"situations"
"in which men use sex"
"as a 'substitute for anger'"

"you're angry at her when she . . .
runs naked in place . . .
because it brings up an earlier
'situation':

your first summer alone
in the country together
in a place where you knew no one"

❧

And she, rising first as always,
would assume a position
naked on the deck
immersed in Gödel and Gordian Knots
in search of "simple and synoptic images"

surrounded by her three inalienable toys:
forest green mathematics textbook,
white legal pad, yellow No. 2 pencil . . .

These three props made her body all the more
erotic—salty beads of perspiration
glistening on her skin,
each drop rolled

one by one
down her belly or back,
dampening her mound
or moistening the crack
between her cheeks.

I took this in with one glance
before I set about fixing breakfast.

♣

This is where representation bows out.

It may have been the dawn
—I can't be sure, I don't know what—
that set off no uncertain trembling.

The stainless steel paleness of that hour.

♣

The sight of her in the light
was more than I could . . . ;

I tried to think about other things,
rummaged in the barbed word *patience* . . . ;

I couldn't keep from coming on,—her
"no, can't you wait till later . . . ,"
                    which she uttered
sharply, not cruelly, with the very tone
that drew me toward her from the outset
made me pursue her against my pattern
of retreat.

When the women you had known
began their domestic fantasy shtick
and cooked you a fatal duck.

Right. One where you didn't have to pick out the buckshot.

Her coolness made me hot.

But you would have the real thing in a mere matter of . . . time.

Lost or found?

Time is only time.

And when did you last imagine it apart from place?

Now. And being here am nowhere.

There is no time. There is only the exhilaration
of a journey: departure is as sexual as light.

She scorned me only when she was working.
That left—when the sun was at its zenith
in the claustral noon
or dusk.

You couldn't wait.
There was nothing to be gained by rushing it.

Either way, I lost.

I can't change how you see the world.

How the world sees me.

☙

But she wasn't posing. She was wagering
that the man with whom she lived wouldn't be
compelled to stare at her when she
withheld nothing from him anyway.

Driving west en route to research she would do concerning
outer space, the possibility
of worlds elsewhere, I was impatient
for the sites of my younger years as well,

nomadic mounds, ricocheting red rock canyons,
roads through eucalyptus groves
toward surfboards and surge;
the billboard announcing the oasis of
Winnemucca, where the underaged males
could yank the handles of slot machines in the urinals . . .

They could not be retraced.

The highway whined its abrasive song of progress.

Struck numb, struck dumb by noon,

yet vaguely turned on from the long hours

so near to her, and by which time

her wet crotch spotted the lightweight khaki-colored

jeans she'd chosen to live in for the journey westward.

(She was always one for uniforms.

Wear one thing and don't waste time
thinking about nothing.)

How many times a day, driving westward,
did I want to say, pull off the road,

let's ignore the burning wind in the cornfields,
or did give in, knowing this woman would say—

"Later! We'll be in—by four."
"But that's four hours from now."
"Too bad. I'm not doing it out in the open."
"But no one will see."
"Can't you take no . . ."

After the time of burning in 117 degrees—
my left forearm and temple still on fire
from the sunset's fierce white radium rays,

I shiver en route to the pool below the sheer
rise of rockface, the flash-flood of stars.

The black water and the night suddenly as cold as each other.

It was the kind of night of which star-charts are made.

❧

THE APPROACH TO LAS VEGAS

Charred mounds laden with the air of migratory creatures.

Dirt roads scratched in around the lone highway
as if desperate men out of low-budget westerns
were clawing the earth
for water.

And out of zero rises—Vegas.
Swathed in whitish dust.

❧

Reaching Vegas, we chose The Sands
for its voluminous pool and auspicious history,
swam, showered, got between the sheets,

—repeated the sequence—

staying in water as long as our skin could take it
before taking the next step toward
entering the casino.

The restaurant's aquarium swarmed
with freshly flown in fish, which we ate,
amazed it could taste so good

in such a wholly artificial atmosphere.
Gigantic behind glass, the sea-
creatures cruised the prison

where they lived out their hours with no relief
from electric light—or from being watched
by awestruck tourists, some of whom

had never traveled out of their home
state except to board a plane and come
here.

᛭

Gamblers, like wrestlers seeking to get a grip
and an advantage before they begin
grappling, loosen up their torsos and arms

at the slots—ignoring the hopeless odds against—
then hone their concentration on the Wheel:
glitter of silver, well-wrought.

(Follow the ball. It's akin to meditation.
Sounds more like mind-control to me . . . hypnosis . . .
If you're looking for trouble we can oblige.)

I pocketed my small winnings at Blackjack
and could not pull her away from the crap
table

to come to bed.

How out of place she looked—
copper skin flush against the multifarious
turquoise of her summer shift,
as if its material, *più pienamente,* had absorbed

the topaz we had poured over in Taos;
erect posture, quiet demeanor—

among the sweaty, grizzled, heavy-lidded

     gamblers

the gallery of types throwing the dice

2

End of August: The Return

Driving north from cloudless Santa Cruz
past straw grass and marshes
with the air-conditioner on full blast
we couldn't keep from heating up

the car en route to Moffet Field
where she would deliver her climactic talk
on how close she had come
to tracking life out there, to receiving a single

signal from the vast silent spaces,
which never cease to terrify
like the California summer's run
of blue stasis in the heights.

She was nervous and you were nervous for her.

Everything was tinged with the melancholy of departure.
The end of summer foaled the beginning of danger.

Goldenrod spread like lit fuses on their way
toward igniting the forest. Bore into fear.

The cattails fretted *tsk tsk tsk*
like old people on call in hospital waiting rooms.

Cicadas clicked at the shrill hysterical pitch
of telephone wires in a mistral.

In other words, there was more.

Having healed so much between you
there was still the earth to mourn.

When you got to the motel she wanted to shower.

I couldn't let her do it alone.

After the glare and dust of the drive.

Her summer dress like having nothing on.

Her consenting, unpredictably, to shower with me.

Her peremptory rubbing of a towel through her hair.

Her undoing the turban she had begun to wind
until we were done with our time of abandon
under the cool, crisp, white motel sheets.

Working up a sweat with the air-conditioner on full blast.

Then showering again.

Never sated, I still watched her stand before the mirror
and drag her wide-toothed comb through her wet hair.

(Twisting the amber handle to loosen snags.)

Another woman might have reacted screamingly
and said *how can you think about that when I'm about to . . .*
how would you feel if our roles were reversed?

Enough of the erotic. Get to her talk.

It's so much easier to say what makes something bad,

or "what went wrong in a relationship"

than to praise without becoming fulsome,
or all too general like a rock song, even a good one,
without violating the subject.

You won't even . . . try?

Words stop short of what it felt like to watch
her put forth, and always with stately
carriage and as few words and flourishes

as possible, the gist of her group's discoveries;
to fill the vast domed auditorium
with minimal concession to academic foreplay,

wafting with her left hand her laser pointer across
the various grids, charts, maps, and graphs;
or keep her poise when reaching for chalk

that wasn't there, and having to ask twice for it;
or to stand alone caged in silence on the bare
stage—with gestures—such as extreme

stillness, I alone in the audience would snare
as anxious, until the slide
projectionist, half-asleep at his post, finally

flashed the right image onto the screen
so she could isolate the telling detail:
scatter—with a resemblance to the dust

of stars that was almost unfair—
signifying why no messages were coming in,
and couldn't come anywhere near for more light years

than I care to consider: considering that words
stop short of what we won't be here to hear
the universe reveal, unravel, or conceal.

❧

Postscript

It—turned you on to watch?

If that's what you're getting out of this I'm lost.

You're no stranger to being lost.

Or you to getting everything backwards!

The tension we felt upon departure had gone,
like a blackbird rising out of the reedy wastes.

You felt it—lift?

Palpably. It left my soul as a virus leaves the body.

173

IV

❦

ABOVE AND BELOW

ABOVE AND BELOW IN MEXICO
(SEEN FROM THE ELEVENTH STORY)

I

I looked out over Mexico City's notorious skyless skies,
and I looked further and the distances contracted to a fist.

Diverging currents of traffic;
skies without ocher and ultramarine.

Over the jagged faded silhouette of the city;
propane tanks perch like pigs at a trough on the rooftops.

Five years ago the earthquake, five years ago my son was born,
and now my horoscope, which I only read when I am traveling,

tells Sagittarians not to twist themselves
during this pantomime of colliding worlds.

I saw Madelaine gracefully coping as Sam gamboled
among the pyramids or extorted presents for putting up

with our desires, and I thought of the banyan trees and the palms,
and the leafy fronds reaching, and the flowery mouth of the god,

and the wild and florid headdresses, jaguar and serpent and bird,
inextinguishable passion, travelers

traveling to uncover that site within themselves,
and I felt a balanced calm whose source I could not remember.

2

The story of the 11th story, from which my father hurled himself,
becomes for me part of other stories where history and myth fuse,

stories of the Toltecs and the Mixtecs, the Aztecs and the Zapotecs,
with their harsh consonantal clatter; the stories of

the Olmecs and the Mayans, of Monte Albán and Mitla and Yaagul,
of Uxmal and Chichén Itzá;

the story of Mexico as "told" by Rivera, Orozco, Siquieros,
and the story of everything that, when I was here before,

had not yet passed into legend,
like the ruins uncovered in the city's center, the zócalo,

the tomb where the privileged skeleton lies,
decapitated legs spread wide and broken at the hip.

The builders on the roofs, slowly reconstructing,
the workers on the sites, slowly reconstructing,

because the deconstructed cities have come to an end,
and it is all right, the time has come to build again

in the open spaces of the ruined buildings, earthquake gutted,
the floors stacked like vertebrae.

3

I looked at the light burning off the smog
and the air growing clear enough to see

and though I couldn't see the mountains through the haze
I knew they were there—and it was good—

and at five in the afternoon the gods herded us out of the ruin—
and Sam called the pigeons wheeling over the zócalo *rats*—and it was
    good—

and there is no way to return because there's nothing to return to.
I admired the order in the chaos of the cars in the multiplying lanes.

The hyperventilating bus passes a clinic curiously marked "Traumato-
    logia."
The German medical student next to me says it has "something to do
    with the brain."

Everywhere mounds of tires rise to the sign "Vulcanizadora,"
(I wish I knew what it was, I'd like to get it done),

and I imagine vultures, *zopilotes*, stock omens of death,
not Hephaestus at his forge—.

4

The bus went by palm trees on the boulevard wound with leather
    pouches,
and mountains and hills beyond which the air is clear

and graded, layered mountain ranges,
and brightly colored steel water bubbles on the rooftops,

and the aluminum factory shining in the noon light,
and factories closed long before five in the afternoon.

When a man boards waving a fan of pamphlets yelling herbal
remedies for everything, everyone digs into their pockets

as we pass the freshly minted suburban mall
where Americans can mix at *Denny's* and feel "at home."

5

Americans picking up *The News* can breathe easy again.

"The Air Force disclosed that its B-2 stealth bomber
has the radar signature of an insect, virtually invisible."

Mexicans picking up *The News* can breathe heavily again.

KILLED

"The body of international relations expert, Celia Ortiz Rojas, 27,
was found when garbage collectors saw blood oozing from a cardboard
    box."

This is not the land of Dreiser and Disney,
and while I lay in bed with the *turistas*

after lingering too long at the ruins,
despite the warning of the sun,

or my human son's incantatory
can we go now, I'm burning . . . ,

reduced to Disney Channel, piped into our room by proud satellite
    dishes,
I realized we'd been duped by this bleak determined vision all these
    years.

I look back twenty years to when I was twenty.
I look ahead a hundred years when not one of us will be here.

The lucid dreams of all I want not to think about trouble my sleep, even
    as I try to intervene,
and I wish they would stop, because I have come here to rest.

And as we breakfast under the arbor's burgeoning bougainvillea,
and our waiter sets a golden mound

of cornflakes before his blond
head, Sam relates his dream: he shot

the leaf's head off because it pulled down
his cardboard chaps; and then it was a quiet evening.

6

There's one tall bare tree in the ploughed field
where the other trees are small and broad and leafy,

and paradoxical shacks—roofs, no doors; doors, no roofs—
and tawny horses grazing among pylons;

and behind, the great mounds wait,
like the pyramids, ringed by mountain ranges,

images of duration endured,
and the sky, darkening as far as any horizon,

and the bunched yucca and cacti which mimic our relentless thirst,
and the almost colorless sandy green hills spiked with maguey,

and the thunder clap and the thunder plane,
and the temple of the sun and the temple of the moon,

above the posthumously named Avenue of the Dead,
and the white deserted stadium in the nowhere with its clear lettering,
    "Contra la **Muerte**!"

and the rows of corn zigzagging like the Mixtec mosaics—
the beaded turquoise skulls icepicked like Trotsky's . . .

7

An ice cream vendor pushes his cart, marked OASIS,
up the narrow, dusty street, into the noon sun;

the peddler wants my Mets hat
more than an "authentic" Aztec statuette,

(Tlaloc the rain god and it was just
starting to rain), and the child pipes down the valleys

wild with his 8,000 peso turtle whistle,
picking his way over the steps without falling.

The 1,000,000+ peso pigskin shoulder bag briefcase
I looked at in the window of the fashionable shop in Mexico City

goes for more than a roof on stilts, tin and tar,
on a ledge in a gorge below Monte Albán:

stick-thin women in single file carry kindling out of the deep
ravine; old men with bandaged arms lug stones down the mountains.

8

After each vertiginous ascent I try to rest
in Oaxaca, the valley of acacias.

Her city, Our Lady of Solitude.
A young boy goes by on a bicycle balancing two

pink blocks of volcanic stone on his handlebars.
Scarlet tanagers settle in the jacaranda trees,

and jubilant roars fill the zócalo,
a rally—placards—**"Viva La Libertad de Expresion"**—

and the police, armed with Uzis, stand by
spitting and sullen, itching for action. . . .

At dusk, while the green stone glows,
I turn my back to cathedrals and cafes,

to the vats of fly-infested pulque,
to the wicker baskets brimful with dark, gnarled roots and branches,

to white metal benches and high wrought-iron balconies,
to multitudes of saints, and beasts, and cherubs,

and walk toward the scattered lights in the hills
where the moon rounds over the Go Kart track,

almost diaphanous, like a palimpsest of clouds
above Monte Albán, where the digging never stops;

a hawker perched on the highest step of the battlements
shoots at rabbits with an empty slingshot

and at those who go on orbiting the stelae—;
a figure squats to give breach birth to a coyote,

and the prisoner's hands are intricately knotted behind his back;
where, because the light was damaging, I spent

the afternoons in search of coolness in the tombs.
The Olmecs knew if they dropped the ball the sun would fall.

And as the bus yaws, losing its hold on the mountain road, the ravine
    yawns,
and I'm staring at a cemetery of turquoise and canary yellow

graves, as if death were a holiday attraction.
There was a time before all this happened,

and sometimes it is good to remember that.
Even destroyed gardens can be destroyed.

Notes

II. The Millennium Hotel

The "real" Millenium Hotel in lower Manhattan is spelled with one "n." Elsewhere I have the usual spelling.

4. "Gambit" is from the X-Men Blue Team. Cyclops describes him *on his card* as "a wild card, a loner. Like Wolverine when he first joined, much of his past still a mystery, Gambit's unpredictability also makes him an asset in our struggles."

"Rain of Arrows at the Dawn of Memory": Most of the "adaptations" in this book stay fairly close to the original, but in this case I have adapted an idea or cluster of ideas so that "after Goethe" refers not to any poem of his, but to a fascinating and controversial early memory: that of emptying the cabinets of his house and throwing all the crockery into the street. Freud, in his intriguing essay on Goethe's childhood, suggested that this might be a screen memory, disguising familial tensions, and having to do with sibling rivalry. In transforming this layered text to a poem of an only child, despairing of the possibility of attention, who at four lives alone with his mother in a high-rise in Manhattan, I substitute toy arrows for crockery, and turn Freud's idea of screen *memories* once again into actual screens.

14. Malcolm Lowry, *Under the Volcano*

III. Motel En Route to "Life Out There"

"Set Design:" The opera referred to as *Faust* is a conflation of several operas, among them *Boris Godunov.*

"Motel En Route to 'Life Out There:'" *più pienamente;* Dante, *Inferno,* Canto XXXII, 5. Other allusions to Dante are suffused throughout the section.

UNIVERSITY PRESS OF NEW ENGLAND publishes books under its own imprint and is the publisher for Brandeis University Press, Dartmouth College, Middlebury College Press, University of New Hampshire, Tufts University, and Salzburg Seminar.

ABOUT THE AUTHOR

Poet, essayist, and translator, Mark Rudman's recent books include *The Nowhere Steps*, a long poem; *Rider*, which received the National Book Critics Circle Award in Poetry for 1994; and *Realm of Unknowing: Meditations on Art, Suicide, and Other Transformations.* He is Guggenheim Fellow for 1996/97. He lives with his wife and son in New York City.

LIBRARY OF CONGRESS CATALOGING-IN-PUBLICATION DATA

Rudman, Mark.
  The Millennium Hotel / by Mark Rudman
    p. cm. — (Wesleyan Poetry)
ISBN 0-8195-2229-5 (cl : alk. paper).—ISBN 0-8195-2230-9 (pa : alk. paper)
I. Title. II. Series.
PS3568.U329M55 1996
811'.54—dc20   95–26572
∞